TRAIL DUST
AND
SADDLE LEATHER

I dedicate this book to Joey ~
my son, companion of many trails,
and a top hand with a horse.

Jo Mora

TRAIL DUST
AND
SADDLE LEATHER

by

Jo Mora

Illustrations by the Author

University of Nebraska Press
Lincoln and London

First Bison Book printing: 1987
Most recent printing indicated by the first digit below:
1   2   3   4   5   6   7   8   9   10

Library of Congress Cataloging-in-Publication Data
Mora, Joseph Jacinto, 1876–1947.
   Trail dust and saddle leather.
   Reprint. Originally published: New York: Scribner,
1946.
   "Bison books."
   1. Cowboys—West (U.S.) 2. West (U.S.)—Social life
and customs. I. Title.
F596.M68 1987   978   86-19303
ISBN 0-8032-3114-8
ISBN 0-8032-8145-5 (pbk.)

Reprinted by arrangement with Jo N. Mora

PREFACE

In presenting this book to the public, I assure you I had no high ambitions of the belles-lettres brand as my incentive. I'm sure that will be quite evident to you if you read on.

A great wave for "riding Western on Western-broke horses with Western rigs" is sweeping the country. Today you'll find rodeos well patronized in the extreme East, and the fiesta silver-mounted stock saddle is no stranger in that fringe where but a few years ago most folks there only knew that Cowboys rode on a big, funny sort of cradle with a great, round, flat-topped doodad sticking up in front. Though half of them did not know whether this was used as an emergency field writing desk or a permanent tray for their afternoon tea when exacting range duties kept these semiwild muchachos in the saddle.

It was to clear up so many of these natural misconceptions, and to answer ever-increasing requests to describe in greater detail the various tools and accoutrements of the cowboy, with their genesis and evolution, that I was spurred on to write and illustrate this book.

All these tools and ways with horses have been part and parcel of me for many years of my life. In these days of gasoline on land and air and water, I still have a long hitching rail under the pines within fifty feet of our garage entrance; and a palomina nickers at me over the rail pasture fence for a lump of sugar but twenty feet away from our great front window.

However, please bear in mind that I'm heading no stampedes nor scratching a bronc for breakfast at my tender years, although I pray that good old Gabe when he takes down his saxophone, or whatever it is he uses these days, to give me the clarion call for that last inspection will let me ease into the saddle with my boots on and jog to that rendezvous.

If I have erred in some small detail—and to err is human—it's not that I have slipped in describing this or that which I may have heard about, but simply that I have viewed the subject through "different eyes." And you know all folks do not have the same viewpoint. Anyhow, I have sincerely set things down as I have seen and known them in the past and know them at the present. I hope you'll like what I offer you.

Adios,

Jo Mora

Monterey, March 18, 1946

ILLUSTRATIONS

TRAIL DUST
AND
SADDLE LEATHER

I

doubt if there has ever been a human character, throughout the ages, to serve as the inspiration for more literature, good, bad, indifferent or execrable, than the American Cowboy. The true United States Cowboy, if we except the old-time California Vaquero, has not as yet celebrated his one hundredth anniversary. And yet, in spite of his tender years, he holds all records for literary material without any competition. Soldiers and sailors from all the ages; kings, queens, pirates and conquerors; lovers and knaves from time immemorial; none have been able to give him a real rush for top honors. Just think of the thousands of stories that have been written and are being written about this character. Think of the scores of current magazines published that are devoted exclusively to "Westerns." Think of the continuous, unbroken series of Cowboy Movies that are produced year in, year out. You just can't beat this hombre for appeal: he's sure nuf got what it takes!

Of course, if we try to figure out what he has in such large measure that gives him this great appeal, we must assuredly cast our vote for the pony he rides. This, naturally, makes him a cavalier, and, as far as that goes, one of the greatest that ever loped into the spotlight. Yes, that must be the touchstone; at least in very great measure, for there is nobody can outshine the man on a horse. Yet, be that as it may, it's a grand record for just a common, ordinary, working man: one who smelled very horsey at times, was generally bowlegged, dunked his doughnuts, gulped his grub, picked his teeth in public, slept in his

1

underwear, and was subject to boils and dyspepsia the same as any other brave working lad.

But the inspired cowboy writer who too often had never been west of Chicago, or St. Louis, generally molded this very human personality as handsome as a Greek god, tall and willowy, and always speaking with that low, lazy drawl that so well belied the lightning speed of his "draw" and the split-second accuracy of his trigger finger. A modern knight-errant, protector of frail or persecuted womanhood, a terror to the evildoer. Ay de mi, que hombre!

If poor old Don Quixote could come to life and pipe the Westerns on the screen, or devour the modern Cowboy stories, he'd soon realize that the gallant old Knights of his feverish, mad dreams were but pikers stacked up to this gay Caballero, Oh, well, we've got to believe in Santa Claus at times to keep our imaginations active and avoid dropping into the robot class. So why get too critical? The old-time cowboy has gone, anyhow; gone with the Dodo and Democracy. Modern writers get about more these days, and with the Dude Ranches mushrooming all over the old West, maybe we'll get a more consistent and realistic picture, at least of the up-to-date Dude Wrangler.

Apart from fiction, a few excellent books have been written about the Cowboy, the history of the Cattle Industry, and the evolution of the Cow Country. The interest on the part of the public at large for these subjects is still very keen, and I have personally had ample proof of this time and time again. A few years ago my son published a poster carte of mine on the evolution of the Cowboy in full colors; and since then we have had countless inquiries for further and more detailed information on his working tools, his clothes, his horse, and his methods of working stock. The limited available space on that carte had forced me to picture and describe my subjects only in the briefest possible manner. Ninety percent of my inquiries are for more descriptive text in place of the simple titles. Here are samples of the questions I get: If a hackamore hasn't a bit attached, how can you control and break a colt with it, or why do they call it a bronc gear? Is a mecate hair rope better than a rawhide reata for general roping?

Well, if the public is sufficiently interested in these subjects to write in for more information, it seems to me that a more detailed edition in book shape should be well worth while. I'll just try to take up where I left off, and hope you will find enough within these covers of interest to make it well worth your time for the reading. There is no fiction within these pages, at least not to my knowledge, and I'll also admit that I don't know it all. But listen, brother, if you're hungry for the truth, just fight shy of the hombre that does know it all.

However, unless I've been blind these many years, I should know a little about it, for, hard as the pill may be to swallow, I'm getting to be what you might call an old-timer. I got my first hard spill in an equine argument fifty-seven years ago when I was an immature twister of ten; and though I'm still in the saddle, I sure enough try to pick the quiet ones these days. But I have had a grand chance to work and observe with Cowboys and Vaqueros from Canada to Tierra Caliente in all these intervening years. Yes, I can remember when there were still old buffalo chips to be found on the plains to make a branding fire; when we used to do our day's work on half-pint mustangs; and I've seen the modern methods creep in, till now when we stuff our saddle horses into trailers after an early breakfast and work stock on them forty miles away, or more, by sun-up.

Boy! That would have sounded like the Arabian Nights and the Magic Carpet to us old-timers when we were young. And yet, to have observed this evolution and taken part in it has been an experience that helped make life worth while and interesting to me. I'm mighty thankful I knew the West before it wore a derby and manicured its fingernails; when there was yet free land for a pioneer; when we were still a young, raw, robust, growing Republic; when our intelligentsia had not

3

yet taken up Karl Marx, and our horse and buggy Constitution clicked.

Now, get me right on this: I'm not one of those old-timers who harp on "the good old days" as the models of perfection. Far from it. We were young then and had growing pains, and these same were often plenty pestering, and positively shameful; and subjects for amputation; for we were only human after all, and Man is the most selfish and cruel example of the Animal Kingdom. But so much elbow room made us recklessly careless. And yet, you didn't find underfoot so many transparent, pink salamanders spewing poisonous foreign isms. You'd generally uncover such things only when you rolled an old log over for firewood at the river bottom. Aw, shucks! I guess that's perfectly natural. Overcrowd your range and I don't care how good the grass may be there in the Spring, you are going to gather some wolf-bait dogies at the Fall round-up.

Anyhow, I'm presenting this book to you for your possible pleasure, information, or to raise an argument over, if you're interested in Cowboys past and present. I'll confine my efforts to just cowboys of the United States; the Mexican Vaquero, who rates a volume all to himself, I may leave for another venture.

What's in a name? Cowboys, Cowpunchers, Cowpokes, Cowhands, Cowmen, Cattlemen, Punchers, Bucaroos, Vaqueros, Waddies, etc., etc. Well, all the names that commence with Cow are self-explanatory. Puncher is a very much used term, though how it ever came to stick and be accepted by the cowboy, is mighty hard to explain. A puncher was a man or a boy with a long pole who generally rode on the cattle trains to punch or prod the "cows" that were down and make them get up on their feet, thus eliminating the danger of being trampled by their traveling mates, and also to goad them along in loading or unloading. This same puncher might be a cowboy, or a farmer, or a dude, or an ordinary bum picked up for the occasion. However, the name has stuck, and it's a most accepted term.

4

Bucaroó or bukéro is only an Anglicized version of the Spanish "Vaquero," meaning cowman. Waddie is a term much used, especially in the old days, and comes from wad . . . something that fills in . . . a man that fills in and completes an outfit. This always sounded like a far-fetched definition to me, but it seems to be the only one I ever found accepted on the old range.

The first thing many people ask is how long the American Cowboy has existed and how he came into being. Lots of folks think that, like Topsy, he jes' growed. Well, he did come mighty near doing just that. Of course, we've had herders of stock from time immemorial, and there's no denying it's one of the most primitive of crafts, if not *the* most. However, the true United States Cowboy is not quite one hundred years of age yet.

Our first real cowboys were Texans, and they learned all the fine arts of the cattle business from the Spaniard or the Mexican. The art of working and handling stock in open country with the aid of well-reined ponies, a noosed rope, and a branding iron, is an American institution and American only. Yet bear in mind, that when I say American, I refer to *all* the New World; for it was first invented, practised, and perfected by the Spaniard in Mexico after the Conquest of those vast lands.

It was way back in the good old days of 1519 that the famous Hernán Cortés, with a mere handful of human hellcats and a very few ponies, landed in Mexico, burned his ships to preclude the possibility of any sissies in his outfit getting homesick, and proceeded to conquer that heavily populated and militarily well organized land of Montezuma. To be exact, his expedition consisted of 110 mariners, 553 soldiers, and—now get a load of this—16 horses for those front-line cavalry shock troops. There's a conquering army for you!

This may be no place to delve into the details of the Conquest of Mexico, which, to my way of estimating, was one of the greatest, most "impossible," wild-cat sporting events in all history. However, mention

5

must be made of it, as it was the very source of the Cow-game in America. Prior to the landing of Mr. Cortés and the merry lads who, more or less, took orders from him, there was not a pony or a cow on the American Continents.

Now, the Cross generally follows the Sword; and the Plough generally follows the Cross; so it wasn't long before garrisons, missions, and pueblos sprang up all over Mexico. Well, the soldados, padres, and pobladores couldn't operate forever on native tortillas, venison and buckskin for their steady meat and leather supply. The white man must have beef and cow leather. Therefore long-horned Spanish cattle were introduced and they found those lush ranges just what the doctor ordered. The way they multiplied was a marvel! There were no fences in this virgin land, and the overflow from the home corrals took to the open ranges, gradually scattered far and wide, and got as wild and spooky as all critters do when freedom is thrust upon them.

In the old country, the Spaniard, who has always been a good stockman, worked his cattle on more or less restricted pastures, with well-reined ponies, a long pike, and quiet bell cows and steers to wheedle the wild ones into doing what they didn't think they were doing. . . . Well, that's one way of working cows, but you've got to have a limited range and some fencing for that method: all of which could not be had on those wild, limitless expanses.

Something had to be done about it, and Mr. Don scratched his head plenty in trying to solve the problem that was really getting away from him. He could not afford to take down the old arquebus and go on a big game hunt every time he wanted a mess of beef for the family puchero, which, without refrigeration, was almost a daily necessity. Well, he messed around one day with his long stake rope, tied a running bowline at one end, built a loop and, in fooling around, hung it on the house pooch as he ran by. Muchacho! That gave him an idea, and he just practised on everything in sight for many days, getting better and better at it all the time. Then one morning bright and early, he saddled up the fastest pony he owned, swung aboard, and jogged out into the hills for the great experiment.

Before long he spied the rangey, brindle steer that always hung out on the edge of the monte, chewing his cud quiet and contented. He eased up to him as close as he could without undue commotion, yet it wasn't long before that steer got a good hunch there was some kind of sheenanigan in the wind, and giving a big snort broke into a trot, and then into his fastest sprint high-tailing it due south for Guatemala. But Mr. Don was ready for that too, and he contacted his pony's ribs with those persuasive gaffs he had strapped to his heels, and the race was on over that rough ground.

That pony was plenty fast and before long ranged up close to his quarry, when the rider quickly built a clumsy loop, gave it a few whirls over his head, and made an amateur's heave in the general direction of that steer's head. It opened up and spilled right over those long horns with beginner's luck, and hung there pretty as a chromo. Caramba! Mr. Don was sure excited by this time, and, without half knowing what he was doing, he snapped up the slack and found himself on that pony going hell bent for election with about eight hundred pounds of wild-eyed beef leading him at the end of his whale line. Then it was that the rider knew just how the bull pup felt when he cornered the wild cat. You know, that feeling of . . . "Well, old boy, you've got what you wanted, now what in heck are you going to do with it?"

But he wasn't given much time to think that over, because the brindle just then changed his mind about the rendezvous, veered sharp to the right, and burned that rope through the rider's hand till it almost smoked. Mr. Don then let go in a hurry, was nearly piled, and kissed his maguey good-bye as he watched it go snaking after that bellowing, jumping steer.

When that Spaniard got over his peeve and got some feeling back

7

into his seared hand, he made up his mind he had really discovered something, yet realized he hadn't gone quite far enough in his research. So he jogged back home doing a heap of thinking. He was satisfied now that cows could be caught with a flying noose from a horse's back, but the catch came when he tried to figure out how he'd hold them after he once caught them.

So it was that he discarded the pad saddle he was riding and got out the old war harness: the saddle with a heavy rigid tree, a high, dished, and partially encircling cantle, and a large, definite pommel on the bow. To this pommel he felt he could fasten his rope, though he did wonder how his pony would stand the shock when the argument got heated and involved. Anyhow it would be worth trying.

As I have just mentioned, the old war saddle had a heavy bow and on it a pommel of many different shapes. This, though it did not have a round stem, gave him ideas, and before long he had altered it into an experimental snubbing post, so that it would not cut or chafe the rope under a heavy jerk with any sharp sides or angles. He figured to take several turns around this doo-dad when the time came to snub.

Well, he blundered along, made a lot of misses and also made a lot of catches. He spilled his pony a time or two, stuck to his purpose, and kept on learning more and more. He cut down and sloped the high, confining cantle to give him more freedom of movement in the saddle, and finally wound up with a working rig that certainly answered all purposes. It was a bit clumsy, perhaps, with its huge "manzana" (apple) in front, but fundamentally the exact rig we ride today. It has just been refined throughout the centuries . . . it has not been changed one bit in principle.

Practice makes perfect, cattle were cheap, ponies plenty, and your Hispano-Mejicano turned into a tip-top operator of the new American system he had invented and was perfecting. And there you have the beginning of the Cowman.

8

JO MORA

However, I must also make brief mention of what developed in these same Americas in those early days, far south of the equator in the Rio de la Plata country. Here the Spaniard was faced with the same problem of handling his thousands of wild cows. He went through the same mental process of developing the noosed rope, but went off on an entirely different tack when he came to the problem of snubbing. He tried to figure out how to fasten his rope to the pad saddle he was riding and did not experiment with a heavy saddle built on a rigid tree. After many experiments and many failures, he realized a saddle was only as strong as its cinch in that type of work. That led him to try an extra cinch passed over the already fastened saddle, like a surcingle, on which was a ring to which he could fasten the end of his rope. This ring came about the middle of the pony's barrel on the off-side. He found this

9

system was decidedly practical and with practice worked to perfection. So that hombre, the Gaucho, developed into a topnotcher of a cowman.

And there you have the two American systems of roping. The Vaquero and the Cowboy working with the horned saddle; the Gaucho with his string tied to a cinch ring. Both of these systems are proven, efficient, and produce masters who can perform marvels. Yet the pommel men think that the cinch operators are a joke and belong in the comic supplements rather than on the range; while the Gaucho, when he feels blue and despondent, just thinks of the Cowboy and the Vaquero for a good laugh which he claims he always gets from these same thoughts. 'Twas ever thus with experts and specialists.

So, let us now go back to the early United States pioneers sifting into Texas, squatting there, and in that vast country learning all about the Spanish ways of handling horses and cows from the resident native Mexicans. The story of the doughty pioneers who later wrested Texas from the Mexicans is a thrilling story of early days and rates a volume of its own; many volumes, in fact. But we must relegate that to its proper place, and dwell here only with the Tejano who has now taken his chosen land from the Mexican. For a brief nine years he made it an independent Republic, and finally was admitted into the Union, which then made him once more a full-fledged United States citizen.

It was quite a primitive, frontier country in those days, and this citizen had learned to break his ponies with a neck rein as did the Spaniard, how to work stock, and how to manipulate the flying loop of the lazo and make it behave in conjunction with his horned saddle. Hard-bitten and individualistic, he modified the Mexican horse gear to his own liking. The native saddle tree was generally covered with very thin rawhide, though often it was uncovered wood, and was fastened to a heavy, large, square leather skirt which had ample saddle bags, likewise square, taking up the entire rear part. Stirrup leathers were wide and without rosaderos, as the large, low-reaching skirt acted as a

10

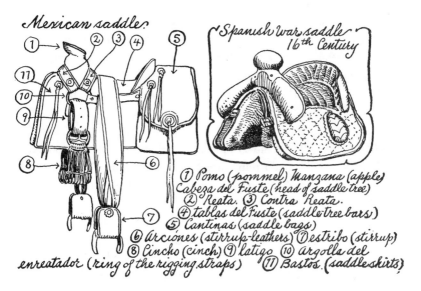

Mexican saddle.

Spanish war saddle. 16th Century

① *Pomo (pommel) Manzana (apple) Cabeza del Fuste (head of saddle tree)* ② *Reata.* ③ *Contra Reata.* ④ *tablas del Fuste (saddle tree bars)* ⑤ *Cantinas (saddle bags)* ⑥ *arciones (stirrup-leathers)* ⑦ *estribo (stirrup)* ⑧ *Cincho (cinch)* ⑨ *latigo* ⑩ *argolla del enreatador (ring of the rigging straps)* ⑪ *Bastos (saddle skirts)*

sweat pad for the rider's legs. It was Spanish rigged: that is, it had but one cinch which hung straight down from the horn. It was secured with very heavy latigos and a tongued ring. I give you here a sketch of a good, average Mexican saddle of the 90's, with the Spanish names for its various component parts.

But our Tejano had ideas of his own, and though the changes came gradually and from various sections of his vast range, little by little the evolution crystallized into a set type of Texas saddle. He changed the big horn to a small one with a narrow stem and small cap. The tree he covered with heavier rawhide, and then covered it all with leather, including the horn. He fastened it to a smaller skirt than the Mexican, and then covered the front and back tree bars with small upper skirts or jockies. Later he covered the side bars with other jockies that passed over the stirrup leathers. The latter he reduced in width and added a

11

sudadero or rosadero (sweat pad) and then discarded the native stirrups. First he used the big, box type, which he called "dog houses," and later to the other extreme with the narrow ox-bows and iron rings. He added a flank cinch to the Spanish rig and so established the double rig.

He didn't fancy the ring or spade bit and took more to snaffles and low ports. The Mexican reins were generally closed and round, plaited or woven, and often with buttons and a romal. These fastened to the bit with chains. All this the Texan discarded and buckled or looped a couple of long, flat, plain reins direct to the bit shank. When he dismounted and left his pony, the reins dropped to the ground, hanging from the bit.

The Mexican was a "Dally man" with his lazo, which was generally of maguey or rawhide, and from him the Texan learned the art of roping. In time, however, this rough and ready hombre felt that this method was too fussy and involved too much artistry in its proper handling. So, he shortened his string, which was generally a grass rope, tied it "hard and fast" to his horn with barbaric indifference and t' hell with the consequences. His worry was only to snare his critter and hold him tight without any argument; after that he'd take his chances on handling him.

The popular Mexican spur was a heavy one that fitted to the *heel* of the *boot*. But these the Texan would not wear on a bet. He made his lighter, of varying designs, but to strap higher up fitting to the *heel* of the *foot*. This type made it perfectly comfortable to walk around with whenever this human centaur condescended to turn into a self-propelled biped. So there is a brief, rough sketch of the early Texas outfit. Later on we'll take it up in greater detail.

Of course, a lad has to have cows around to be a cowboy, and believe me those Texas ranges had them aplenty: leggy, wild-eyed, long-horned Spanish cattle. They just seemed to fit on those mesquitales and they increased rapidly. It didn't take much beef to furnish our pioneer with his fresh meat, his tasajo (jerky or dried meat) and his pickled stock. His main problem developed into what was he going to do with all these fast-increasing herds that were eating up his range and not making him any richer. A market had to be found, but conditions and environments were very primitive out there in those days. Business had to be done without much rural postal service, no telegraph, no telephone, no wireless; and cattle had to be transported on the hoof hundreds of miles over difficult, rough, often waterless terrain, teeming with all kinds of natural and human hazards. There was no refrigeration in those days, and you just had to herd your fresh beef to market by its own locomotion.

They did finally work out some avenues of commerce to the Gulf where sailing and steam freighters took on limited numbers for outside domestic and foreign markets. To New Orleans, Mobile, and Florida; as also to some of the slave-working islands of the Caribbean, such as Cuba, Puerto Rico, etc. Then some of the more adventurous made long drives to the Mississippi River for other water-shipping outlets. Others of that ilk tried out the trails to the northern market, which were then but little known and very hazardous. Those pioneers were just feeling out the possibilities, for they had to find an outlet. However, all these were difficult, dangerous ventures, and they tapped only a small fraction of that great supply which was steadily increasing season by season. It soon got to the point where a Texas stockman's poverty was reckoned by the number of cattle he owned. The more he had, the poorer he was.

Then came the great Civil War, and Texas naturally cast her lot with the Confederacy. Most of her able-bodied men went to the war, but the cattle at home kept right on increasing in numbers. The comparatively small consumption of beef by those staying behind, and the losses by Mexican and Indian raiders were negligible. Some beef was utilized by the Confederacy, but the Union Army was able to cut off from use any great avenue of supply to the warring army or to the civilian population.

When Appomattox finally sounded taps to the great struggle, the battle-weary Texans drifted back to an impoverished homeland. And yet it was teeming with thousands on thousands of longhorns which, without proper markets, might almost be listed as liabilities instead of assets. There had been mighty little supervision and branding for five years, and these critters roamed the brush as wild and spooky as deer. Three or four dollars a head would have been an average price for the best, but who was there to give it? And yet, at this very same time, conditions were exactly the reverse in the North and the East, for there they had only a limited supply of beef and prices soared sky-high. Nice thick beefsteaks were not the regular diet on the tables of the middle-classes and the poor.

So then the Texan, trying to work out his own salvation, started up some "factories" to specialize in hides and tallow and salted beef. These products they figured would be easier to handle and ship than great herds of wild cattle. Most of these plants were located on the Gulf coast, accessible to shipping facilities. The idea took hold right from the start and proved very practical; and, like most all our successful movements, when folks saw things were going well, the boom was on, and everybody within hail elbowed to climb on the band-wagon. There was a mad, wholesale rush to kill cattle. Thousands were slaughtered for their hides, tallow and some meat for salting; thousands for their hides and tallow; and still thousands for their hides alone. The prodigality of that slaughter was typically American, and the range commenced to stink with the odor of rotting carcasses.

The very fact that there existed certain very generous laws controlling the cattle industry helped work matters out in the reverse of their intended purpose. Instead of controlling they helped create greater

Old time Texas "Skinning Outfit"

abuses, all of which got out of hand finally and resulted in what was termed the Skinning War. Before that time, anyone was entitled to the hide off a dead cow on finding such, regardless of the brand it carried. These were called "fallen hides," and it was legitimate for one to take this hide just as one might brand a maverick (unbranded cow) and claim it as one's own.

Overstocking the range caused many losses when the bad weather came, and also many cattle drifting down before heavy storms into the bayou country of the coast, bogged down and died in countless numbers. There was free skinning with a vengeance! Then, like all such mad rushes, abuses crept in and soon commenced to assume abnormal proportions. When not sufficient dead cattle were found to make it worthwhile, the skinners helped many a live one along to the Happy Grazing Grounds with a lead slug where it would do the most good.

Before this new rush developed into such a stampede, the skinning of dead cows, "die-ups," was looked forward to as perfectly natural and

15

called the Skinning Season on the low coast ranges. This occurred in the winter. Of course, the owners of the cattle did not particularly revel in the yearly prospects, yet took it as just one phase of the cattle business in that section; and, as many of these cows were from other ranges and had drifted down, they added a little to the yearly income and helped make up for the losses among their own stock. The small ranchers, however, and the backwoods settler and squatter whose annual income from a small and uncertain corn and razorback crop didn't rate the financial columns, naturally looked forward to the Skinning Season as a boon and a welcomed means of getting a little money from the hide crop.

The coming of the hide and tallow factories where a readier, handier market for hides was to be found, helped considerably in boosting the popularity of the Skinning Season. This, in time, grew to quite alarming proportions. And don't think this was just a little local incident, for the slaughter spread farther back from the immediate shores of the Gulf when the pickings there got slender. It spread well inland to the higher prairies and brush country, taking in a large territory from the Rio Grande to the Sabine. Some of these free-shooting, thieving outfits got pretty well organized, too, with pack animals and even oxcarts to transport the hides when the killings and skinnings were quite distant from the factories.

So, I think you will readily agree that it was perfectly natural for the owners of those cows which were succumbing in such large numbers to this prevalent lead poisoning, to get a little hot under the collar themselves and decide to do something about it and join in the merry shooting match, not caring where the bullets might land. Well, the answer to all this was that a heap of careless lead went whizzing through that lazy Texas ozone, and the Skinning Season turned into the Skinning War. There were quite a few casualties, and they weren't all cows by a long shot. And yet, in spite of all this fuss, the export of hides, tallow, and salt meat from the Gulf was immense, and really commenced to relieve the tough economic situation of that post-war, poverty stricken Texas.

But all the activities of the stockmen were not turned solely in the direction of the Gulf for an outlet. Many large trail herds were made up immediately after the war, for another try at the northern markets. With all the discouraging, evident hazards in view, and the impossible local prices, there were still many courageous drovers who were convinced that there *had* to be a market for their cattle away from home, and they were willing to gamble with everything they had on the issue. They had the courage of their convictions and were willing to risk them, make or break. You can't stop men who figure that way; and it's gamblers on the future that make history.

So, in the Spring of '66, many herds which had been made up for that year's gamble, took to the trails for the North, and thousands of longhorns crossed the Red River heading for Kansas. At the Indian Territory, they ran into considerable trouble with the Redmen who resented the crossing of their lands by such large herds, and also felt a natural desire for remuneration from the drovers for the grass cropped off by those vast numbers. Some of the drovers paid toll, others argued and had trouble, and most of them veered over to the east and quartered to come out into the State of Arkansas. There they had to turn again sharp to the north to avoid the rough foothills of the Boston Mountains which was not good country to negotiate with a large trail herd of spooky cows. They kept on till they struck southwest Missouri, and, further on, southwest Kansas. Space allows me only to touch the high spots of that epic, the Texas drive of '66, just to show you in a most sketchy way that it was not all molasses and white biscuits and romance with those intrepid drovers.

To get a fair idea of what those Texans had to contend with, you must realize that those immense herds of longhorns were made up of the wildest, spookiest critters, short of buffalo and deer, that could be found in the West. After they had been sufficiently broken to stay more or less together under the expert handling and continuous supervision of those cow-wise drovers, a sneeze or an unexpected move might set them off into a frenzied stampede and scatter them to the four winds in that vast, unfenced country.

Just get that condition foremost in your mind, then realize what natural hazards the country to be traversed offered. At that time trails were not well known; feed, in certain sections, was very scarce or non-existent; rivers had to be crossed that might be dry, hock deep, or raging torrents over night; and there were stretches where waterless drives had to be made, pushing on with suffering, wild-eyed, temperamental longhorns into unknown conditions ahead. And sometimes only to be obliged to turn back, in defeat, to recuperate and try by some other route. They certainly had their troubles, yet those just mentioned were only the setbacks of Nature. The Human ones were still to come.

As I have already mentioned, in crossing the Indian Territory, or the Nations, they had the Redman to contend with. Large portions of the Nations were occupied by the civilized Indians, such as the Cherokees, and they had to be dealt with much as one would with white residents under similar circumstances. However, there were also plenty of "blanket Indians" on the loose throughout that land, a land they had been told belonged to them and to which they were confined, and these did not take kindly to the big herds tramping down and eating their grass without some recompense. In all fairness, they were certainly entitled to it. Yet how many whites in those days could judge an Indian fairly?

But those hard-bitten Texans with the big herds were accustomed to sleeping with one eye open, and every morning ran their fingers through their hair to see that it was still there. They were accustomed to trouble and took it all in stride, yet when they got out of the Indian Nations they thought they had at last left the human hazards behind them. And that's where they proved themselves poor guessers. When they came to southwest Missouri and southeast Kansas, they commenced to breathe freely, thinking they were finally free from such recent pesterings and in a white man's country once more. But Old Man Trouble just stalked them plenty and halted them on that hard trail. The Indian menace was kindergarten stuff compared with what they now had to face.

They were met and stopped by as tough and lawless a bunch of cutthroats, thieves, and extortionists as ever merited iron bars. The great hue and cry they set up was that they feared the ticks those longhorns were packing into their fair land to disseminate the dreaded Texas fever among their own cattle. Now, mind you, there were many well-intentioned citizens in those sections that were quite sincere in their protests and antagonism to the Texas herds on that score, and not without some justification. However, these bands of scum and border riffraff that held up those first drovers needed only such an excuse, if indeed they resorted to it at all, to hold up, extort, rob, stampede, and even murder. It was their greater numbers and perfect knowledge of the local country and conditions that helped those ruffians in their nefarious tactics; though they did encounter some pretty determined hombres, and not in all cases did they get away with everything they tried to put over.

However, those drovers were badly impeded in their routine, and herds soon commenced to bank up in that bit of country near Baxter Springs in southeast Kansas, right at the common corner with the Indian Territory and Missouri, and but thirty miles or so from Arkansas. The season was getting late, and some of the drovers turned west along the south Kansas border; some went east into Missouri; and others tried to winter somewhere in the vicinity. A few herds worked through into Iowa and the corn belt, and others found buyers at various places. But, by that time, many of the cattle were in poor shape, and, while a few made a fair profit, the majority fared very badly. Altogether, it had not been a year to encourage the Texas drover to try for northern markets;

19

and when word got back of the holdup methods encountered in Missouri and Kansas, the number of herds to be made up for the next year's try dropped tremendously.

In Government statistics it has been recorded that in 1866, 260,000 Texas cattle crossed the Red River seeking outside markets. Personally, I think this estimate is very low, as I have had access to stockmen's books and diaries of that time, which nearly all placed the number nearer to 350,000. Of course, this is all conjecture at best, for nobody really knows or ever did know. Anyhow, it's a safe bet to say that it was from a quarter million up in '66. But, also estimated, the next year the number dropped to 35,000. The risks had been too great for the results attained.

At this very time, a great juncture was shaping up in the North. The grand era of railroad building was on full swing, and the tracks for the Iron Horse were being laid across this vast Continent from east to west, and from west to east, as fast as Man could overcome the natural hazards encountered. The virgin prairies were the scenes of feverish human activities. Towns were springing up like mushrooms all along the right of way. Crews of railroad workers were slowly inching ahead like great hordes of human ants, ever on, and on, and on, methodically and steadily. Ruthless professional hunters and skinners were exterminating the Buffalo for his hide and some meat to feed this army of workers. It was a pitiable slaughter; and the Plains Indians who depended exclusively on this creature for their food, clothing, and economic existence, were getting very resentful and ready for the war path. The United States Army was sent out to keep them within bounds. Overland trails were being deeply rutted by the wheels of the covered wagons rolling ever westward to the El Dorado of the Pacific. Steadily, unconsciously, these human midgets were shaping up a colossal future. Welders of an Empire and not to be denied.

Now, unromantic as this may sound to the dreamer, the whole situation needed one thing . . . BEEF. The supply of buffalo was nearing extinction, and the army of railroad builders needed beef; and as they slowly extended their railheads westward, they were establishing new facilities by which that same beef might be transported east where it was also so greatly needed. The Indian, no longer able to subsist by hunting, had to have beef; and the soldier, policing those wards of the Government, had to have beef. The demand was imperative, and the solution very evident, for Texas had the great desideratum in prodigious quantities. True, under existing conditions, it was a long way off, but just create a market of more or less stability and a shipping point with some kind of a fair-play guarantee, and all Hell with his cloven-footed satellites couldn't stop those doughty Texans from throwing their great herds on the trail, and, fair weather or foul, driving them smack up to the Promised Land.

I never could see why the Railroads overlooked this prospect even before they commenced laying tracks. Then, too, later on when they were approached with this proposition, many of them turned it down flat as visionary and positively impractical. How silly! Think of shipping thousands of wiggling, bellowing longhorns on a railroad train. Why, the very idea! But the young man who was promoting this idea knew that he had something, and he also had, whether he knew it or not, a lot of dog-goned perseverence, and he hung to his purpose like a puppy to a root. Finally he wore down one Railroad President to the point where he condescended to build a spur and provide facilities where a stock-yard might be placed.

Then when it came time to choose a site for this grand scheme, he had to lick his calf all over again. Community after community turned it down, or asked outrageous prices and conditions that made it impossible. It was plain to see there was plenty opposition to Texas cattle.

However, where there's a will there's a way, and finally the thriving prairie metropolis of Abilene, Kansas, was chosen for the venture in 1867. At that time the town consisted of "about one dozen log huts, small, rude affairs, four-fifths of which were covered with dirt for roofing; indeed, but one shingle roof could be seen in the whole city. The business of the burg was conducted in two small rooms, mere log huts, and of course the inevitable saloon also in a log hut was to be found."

But, once the decision was made, the work began, and in 60 days a shipping yard that would accommodate 3,000 cattle, a large Fairbank's scales, a barn, and an office were completed, and a good three-story hotel well on the way to completion. These facilities were finished on the 5th of September, 1867, and on that day the first shipment of 20 cars was made to Chicago, the first train load of cattle to pass over the Kansas Pacific Railroad.

That year, but 35,000 head of cattle came up the trail, as stated before. It had been a bad year all around with excessively heavy rains and swollen streams, Osage Indian troubles, and an epidemic of cholera. So, add to this the troubles of the previous year and you have a messy prospect. When the Agent, traveling on horseback, met the herds on the trail the next year and told the drovers that Abilene had a stock yard and shipping facilities and wanted their business, he was received with considerable suspicion and frigidity right from the start. Your Texan was not quick to forget, and the recollections of his treatment the previous year still stuck in his crop. The very thought that some blue-bellied Yanks were trying to make it comfortable for him and his herds, and would help him find a buyer, well . . . it didn't smell too good to him, and wasn't easy to swallow. But he was a gambler, first, last, and always, and he'd take a chance. So up to Abilene many of them went, and found it was all as had been advertised. It was true they wanted him as much as he needed them. Buyers were there, and trains ready for shipment. The ice was finally broken. WHOOPEEEEE! The boom was on! Hop along you dogies, north we go! And the era of the great cattle trails commenced.

That was the Golden Age of the Cowboy West. You might say it was

Types of the early Cattle Trails

the very birthday of the Cowboy as a distinct type in America. True, he had been operating in Texas for many years before that, first as a pioneer learning his craft from the Mexican, and later working his own cattle in a more or less aimless sort of way as an adjunct to his other rural endeavors. But with increasing markets for his stock now definitely established, the Long Trails were the proving grounds, the school of the Cowboy. From these he graduated, got his degree, and blossomed into a distinct, new type to the United States. The mature East did not know him, and the new Middle-West met him with great reserve and much antagonism. His breezy, unconventional, reckless, swaggering personality did not exactly fit into the rather strait-laced, psalm-singing viewpoint. When they saw those great hordes of longhorns, with their devil-may-care centaurs in attendance looming up out of the South, they made them about as welcomed as a blight of locusts. But there was no stopping him now. The Long Trails were being slowly and indelibly graved into the virgin sod of the prairies.

The Chisholm Trail, the West Chisholm, the Shawnee, the Panhandle, the Pecos, the Western, the Goodnight-Loving, the Northern, the Bozeman, etc., etc. Nearly all emanated from Texas and afforded an exit, a broad highway for the bellowing thousands of longhorns that fed the East for a time and also took the place of the buffalo on the great open northern ranges of our West.

The most popular of these trails, at least the best known to the outside world, was the Chisholm Trail, named after a half-breed Cherokee, Jesse Chisholm, who first established it as a wagon trail, though it had been, prior to that, routed by a Delaware Indian army scout in guiding a soldier column out of the Indian Territory into Kansas. It certainly established itself in the romance and glamour of the cattle drives throughout the years long after it had ceased to serve its original purpose. Today, in the minds of many, it stands as the epitome and legendary symbol of the great Cattle Trail Era.

So, at last, the teeming thousands of wild-eyed longhorns were an asset and not a liability, and it was getting to be well worth while to own a herd. The chaotic conditions of the Texas range, right after the Civil War, offered a grand chance for smart, or hustling, or opportuning, or thieving individuals to start up in the cattle business. The foundations for many an ample fortune were commenced right then and there; and guts, ropes, and running irons were not the least of the items that started many a lad on the rosy, and sometimes doubtful, path to financial prosperity.

I made no mistake in remarking that there was chaos on the Texas range at the end of the Civil War. Most of the ranchers had been away to the wars, and many had not returned. The affairs of the latter were naturally in a muddle. Things had not been kept up much by the women or those staying at home. There had been little branding and supervision, and the brands were pretty well shuffled up all over the State. Plenty of mavericks and plenty of unbranded cows with calves. It was a wonderful set-up for hombres of easy conscience, and the only thing that helped put the brakes on at the time was the fact that cows were not worth much.

The unwritten laws of that range were simple and loosely thrown together, and based entirely on human honesty for their effectiveness. And they worked out pretty well as long as cows had little value. Branding was done with a running iron, and there were no large, well organized, regular round-ups. There was no necessity for them. A rancher, with his men, rode his own range, branded his own calves and everybody else's that might have strayed into his circle. Just as long as a calf was with its mother beyond a doubt, he marked it with the brand of the mother; and, in doing this, he knew his own strays were being taken care of in the same way.

If he gathered a herd to drive to market and outside cows got into his bunch, he just took them along and sold them regardless. He simply made a record of it and reimbursed the original owner when the time came. For doing this he was allowed to collect $1.00 per head as a fee. Then again, they got into the habit of paying four bits a head for all calves branded by outsiders.

Well, all these things worked out pretty well in a shiftless sort of way. Then some men made it more of a business to brand others' calves just for the four bits per that was in it and not in the regular routine of their own work. But one thing led to another, and mistakes commenced to be made with more regularity. That is, many of the branders just mentioned commenced to get mighty absent-minded and slapped on their own brands instead. Of course, it was all a case of absent-minded-ness, but after it was done it would have been a messy job to try to rectify the error. So they just let it go.

Before long, however, things got pretty raw, and, as usually happens in such emergencies, a flock of laws were made and passed to rectify those loose business methods and try to help certain hombres along into the narrow trail to Honesty. But they got a bit too complicated for the ordinary rancher. It got so one couldn't take a herd out without making a detailed document in duplicate, stating the number of cattle, the various brands and ear markings, the classifications, etc., etc. Then this all had to be inspected and passed by a deputized County Inspector who took the duplicate and filed it at the county seat to be entered in the Stock Book that was always open for inspection to the public. All that red tape must have been a merry picnic to some of those old-timers who had to shove their tongues in their cheeks to write their own names in a legible hand. No, I'm not getting sarcastic: I feel the same way myself when I have to fill out some of the tax questionnaires we get these days.

This was all fine and dandy for a while, and one could go over to the county seat and get the whole story of every herd transaction to the minutest detail, even to prices paid and who sold to whom and whatnot.

I guess it was too good, for those complicated methods work out better on paper than with a lot of back-range cowmen. That was a country of wide open spaces, and you could not always find the debtor or the creditor when you wanted them; and not everybody was good pay; and even if they had been, not everybody had the money when the call came. In trying to simplify matters, certain small cliques worked together with powers of attorney one from another. This worked out fairly well for some and for a while, but it was no "cure all." The trouble was that the open range was too small, vast as it was, for so many hundreds of brands shuffling and reshuffling themselves over that unfenced domain. And with the prices on cows going up, many local hombres got looser and looser with the conscience, and plenty of outsiders sifted in who had never had a conscience, with the result, as already mentioned, of chaos aplenty and hell to pay in general. Plenty of gunpowder was burned, lots of blood spilled, and make no mistake about that.

Now you may be surprised to learn of an item that helped to straighten out matters where laws and gunpowder had failed. I'll not say it did it, presto—chango! over night; but I will say it was the foundation for law and order in the cattle business. This was the introduction of "Bob-wire." Yet what a reception and what an opposition it ran into when it first showed up. That fiendish contraption of the Devil's imagination was going to cut those range cows to shreds. There would not be a sound hide in all Texas one month after that torturing device had been stretched. And how about screw worms? Had anybody thought of that? No, siree! The man that would resort to such a fiendish device ought to be strung up and riddled with lead.

Well, they blew off steam, and then, as always happens, somebody had the courage to try it out and found that the durned thing worked. Bob-wire had come to stay. It had to go through that trying-out period that all radically new inventions must submit to. I've had old-timers tell me of the agitation the coming of the railroads had created, with that Devil's engine belching fire and sure to ruin the wool crop with all its smoke and soot. Did you get that? Ruin the wool crop. Oh, well, as far as that goes, I can remember myself, not so long ago, seeing farmers, in certain rural communities, fighting mad and up in arms, ready to shoot any of those damned city slickers that might dare to invade their backwoods roads with those chugging horseless carriages to scare their teams into spasms, cause runaways, and spread death and disaster on the public ways. Anyhow, barbed wire came to Texas in the later seventies and proved its worth.

Now the open range began to be fenced and a man could control his own cattle, and breed as he wished. There had been no incentive before that to try to improve a herd, because with every old scrub bull in the country having access to any corner of the range that his romantic trend might fancy, what was the use of trying to be particular. But now it was a different story. It made it a trifle harder for the cattle thief, too; though, of course, if that scum could get around existing laws, a good pair of pliers helped him enter that new-found exclusiveness. Yet it *was* different now, and the cattle business commenced to thrive by leaps and bounds.

It had always been known that cows raised in the southern part of the State would put on weight if transferred to the grasses of the northern counties; but it had also been a foregone conclusion that a southern-bred Texas longhorn could not weather the cold and the snows of a real northern winter. Well, that was the next balloon to be busted. So they tried it, and the Texas cows not only weathered a real northern winter on the open range, but, after the Spring grazing, put on weight in a manner that had never been known before. So that settled that, and there was no stopping that longhorned critter from stocking those northern ranges from then on. The latter had been depleted of the buffalo, and, as the Indian was being gradually pacified and corraled,

Those desiccated, sun-kissed Brasaderos had a tough jerk weathering that first northern winter.

JO MORA

the great open spaces and limitless free grass of that Empire between the Missouri and the Rockies offered a cattle range such as the world has never known.

The cattle boom was on now, and swept over that vast land like an avalanche, leaving innumerable new ranches in every advantageous, available locality. The Texas cowboy who had been driving cows to the railroad towns of Abilene, Newton, Wichita, Ellsworth, Fort Dodge, etc., now also pushed on with breeders to stock these new ranges of the North.

The craze to be a cowboy swept the country like wildfire, and adventurous young bucks from the East and the South sought the rolling prairies of the Wild West to satisfy their ardor and heed the precepts of Horace Greeley when he advised, "Go west, young man!" There they met the Texan as ranch foremen and cowboys, and were taught by them the ways of handling cows and horses, just as they themselves had been taught by the Mexicans not so many years before. It was a hard school; an exciting school; a man's school. Evolutions worked fast in the outdoor classes of those days, and so it came to pass that

29

before long the cowboy was no longer a Texan alone, but could trace his origin from all corners of the land and every station in life: high, low, white collar, farm or city slum. He even came direct from foreign lands, yet so potent was that prairie melting pot and so strong the parent root, that in no time they all took on a characteristic that was distinct and vital. He was young and he had to be healthy, pliant, and tough to survive.

The American Cowboy was now a national institution, proud of his calling, conscious of his self-gauged superiority, and, to the outsider, wild and woolly, highly advertised and little understood. His reign was short, colorful and vigorous, for, like all great pioneer movements in this land of ours, when we were still in short pants and the grammar grades, things moved fast; oh, so fast! Yet he stamped the broad land he worked over with a character that the years have not been able to eradicate with all the altering and blending of the plow, the subdivision, the radio, the railroad, paved highways and the derby. The old-time cowboy on his half-pint mustang, the herder of the long trails and the open range has long since gone; the cowboy of today is a worthy successor, but he's a different animal.

I have tried to give you a brief, sketchy picture of the events leading up to and through the evolution of the old-time cowboy. Please bear in mind that I fully realize I have painted this with a broad brush; available space dictates for brevity, and I've had to boil things down to that dangerous minimum where one stands in danger of losing the desired perspective. What a vital American Epic the story of that cattle invasion is! It merits volumes at its every phase.

Anyhow, we now have our cowboy to fuss over, and we can proceed to further pick him to pieces, see how he's assembled, and try to find out what makes the derned thing run.

There's been heaps of definitions coined anent this Cowboy and some of them pretty salty; but too many of them overlook the fact that

Types of the Great Plains   1880-90

JO MORA

a good cowboy is more than a man with guts and a horse, who can rope like a wizard and ride anything that wears hair. Those are mighty potent qualifications and sure enough desirable, but don't overlook that to be a real, top hand buccaroo, one should have, above all else, that natural God-given SOMETHING that's born in one and seldom acquired . . . good Horse and Cow sense. The very best cowboys I've known throughout the years all had that certain SOMETHING, could work stock like magicians, and yet were only average ropers and about as anxious to top off a bronc for breakfast as a duck is to dance on a hot griddle. Yet what efficient cowmen they all were. They could out-guess a cow or a horse, make 'em do pretty near what they wanted them to do without those critters really knowing they had just been made to do something that maybe they hadn't wanted to. It's a gift.

Some so-called cowboys can gather and ride through a herd of range cows or horses, and right from the start will get them all hot and fussed, their own riding ponies in a lather, and the job they started out to do but poorly done, if done at all. Another team can ride in and through them, ease out a snorty steer to the edge, give him a couple of wiggles, and start him off for the beef cut on the run and make him think he did it all on his own account. Same thing with riding down and placing a herd on the bed ground for the night, well spaced out, quiet and contented. Or watering a thirsty herd at a river so they'll string out and get their fill quietly and to advantage. Some men can do it; some can't. A lad might be a tip-top, first money rodeo show bronc rider, and still not know which end of a cow eats; but he can't be an A-1 working range cowboy without that sixth sense.

Some writers in describing those early Texas waddies that went up the Cattle Trails, make the mistake, to my way of looking at it, of trying to build a mold that would fit all of them: just like they were a distinct genus of the human family. The truth is they almost got to be that later on at the peak of their reign, but the very early ones were just a cross section of Texan pioneer humanity, and you couldn't create a type model for all of them no more than you can for college boys, or carpenters, or bell hops.

There were a few large ranch owners who might even be town dwellers part of the time; smaller ranchers and stockmen; those of the back range Hill-Billy type; even poor white trash; and not a few negro hands. There were those of fair education, though, as a rule, "book larnin'" was not their "piece de resistance," and naturally many of them were illiterate. Kids living so many miles from the little old red school houses are not exactly the ones to establish attendance records, especially when those miles were periodically crossed by parties of hair-hunting Indians. Yet many fine individuals, later to hold high positions in life, received their first reading and writing lessons at their mothers' apron strings in little log cabins and sod houses of the far-flung frontier. The rank and file of the waddies that trailed north with the big herds were not exactly in the valedictorian classes. The frontier was crude and elemental and the waddie reflected it. He couldn't be anything else. Then, too, one must add to this pioneer simplicity that extreme alertness necessary to hold one's own in a newly conquered country. This land he had but recently taken from the Mexicans and they resented it deeply, and for many years there was continual raiding and gun play. And also let us not forget the original owners, the Indians. They kept up a desultory warfare against both sides. So I think you will agree that all this tended to make our waddie a very self-reliant and hardy type, if not a great academician. Anyhow, one that wouldn't faint if you yelled "Boo!"

Yet we should not stop here in analyzing the veneer that hardened those waddies. What about that greatest of all conflicts known up to that time, the Civil War? A great proportion of those early trail hands had been tempered in that terrific forge; and we all know that wars of that caliber are not particularly famous for softening the moral fibre of

33

a human being. So, when you add this to a man who was already accustomed to violence and the dire necessity of looking out for himself at all times to keep alive, we get an individual that, barring exceptions, is tough, careless of life, callous to blood and suffering, and . . . well, one you could scarcely call a siss. He might have been a little narrow in his horizons, most borderlanders are, but he had a strong sense of primitive justice, and his word was generally good. He was positively servile to nobody; and yet he could be loyal unto death to an individual, an employer, a brand, or an issue.

So, there's the general veneer we can apply to our early trail hand as he came out of humanity's stock: good, bad, brave, timid, sneaky or arrogant. As a rule, away from home, family, and his women folks, trail life made him careless, hard living, hard cussing, hard drinking when he sought his relaxation, though very seldom an habitual drunkard. In his deference for a decent woman he was shy but all-protecting: her champion to an exaggerated point. The painted female he accepted at her own valuation. Cowtowns at the end of the trails were full of the latter, waiting to snare him; the vast frontier was sparsely sprinkled with the former.

Ever since Man has been Man, the rapacious has hunted the innocent, and the sharper, with his gold brick and knockout drops, has stalked the gullible rube with his carpet bag and roll of frogskins. That's as it has been and always will be. So keep that picture back in your mind as we watch the railroads being built across the Continent, creeping west . . . west . . . west, and the mushroom towns breaking through all along the right of way.

The granger squatted in the outlying districts where the soil and water seemed best suited. The man of commerce, the small merchant, he stayed in the settlement and prayed for customers. The frontier freighter with his jerk-line teams and the packers with their outfits came there to deliver their loads. Buffalo hunters came with their hides, got

beastly drunk and caroused savagely. If near an army post, soldiers joined with the visitors, and the regular flotsam and jetsam of the frontier. Then, to prey on all this varied personnel, the hawkeyed gamblers and the painted ladies made their appearance. They were just following the sucker migrations.

With that picture before us, with the hard-eyed human spiders spreading their webs for the prey, we are ready for the entrance of the innocent rube, the guileless rustic from the brush country. Whoopee! Here he comes now! But does he enter the picture stammering in bucolic embarrassment, rubbing one foot back on the other in apologetic indecision? He does like hell! That unsophisticated sucker comes boiling up Main Street on a steaming mustang, six-guns popping at the stars and splitting the welkin with his rebel war whoop. Good-natured, overgrown boys looking forward to fun and relaxation the only way they knew it. The tiresome, lonesome days on the long trails were finished, and the dangers, the excitement, the possibilities of sudden death had all been in the day's work. Here he was in town, ready for a spree, and the unwitting sucker the hawks were waiting for. Well, there was a set-up that could turn into a volcanic climax at the snap of a finger. You agree to that, will you not? Anyhow, just take it from me . . . it often did.

Those soft-spoken southern boys, so far away from their mothers, considered anybody from north of the Red River, a blue-bellied Yank, and, since the very recent unpleasantness, not a particularly loved individual. As a rule, when in "enemy territory," they were quite on the defensive, a bit touchy, quick to interpret a slight or an insult, and quicker to do something about it. However, let's keep one thing in mind while we're estimating the Texas cowboy of the Cattle Trails. Right after the great war, hundreds of desperate ne'er-do-wells, disillusioned veterans who had bumped into trouble, and habitual criminals fleeing the tentacles of the law in better organized communities, all drifted into the Indian Nations and the vast reaches of Texas where law and order had not as yet commenced to function at its best.

Many of these got jobs on the trail crews and helped to make up the dramatis personae of the wild scenes in the lurid cowtowns at the end of the drives. Naturally, most of these scorpions got into the headlines, and when they did they were classified as Cowboys (and quite naturally) which at that time was synonymous with Texan. There is no doubt that the Lone Star State had to take plenty of undeserved credit for the pyrotechnics of those gutter rats. On the other hand, don't think that I mean by this that there were no naughty boys from Texas mixed up in those cowtown jamborees: far from it. But I will say that there were less real, bona-fide cowboys involved than outsiders. However, everything finds its level in time, and, awaiting the day when law and order could take over, the progressive citizens staked out a little sub-division back of town which was called Boot Hill, and where might be readily planted those enthusiasts who had come west to grow up with the country and had answered Gabriel's sudden call without the formality of taking off their boots.

I'd like to whisper right here that those early cowtowns were tough. And take this from one who has seen tough towns all over the world, old times, modern times, and in-between times. They were hard, riotous, and debauched in anybody's company. Of course, I don't mean to put them up on an untouchable pedestal, hell no! The one thing to their disadvantage was that they were no bigger 'n a peanut, and some of them didn't even have buildings on both sides of Main Street. So, you see, all that pizen was concentrated into a small space, like an extract or an essence; and as there was not much beside the tough part, it was magnified that much more. The truth is they were not a bit worse than some of the slums of London, or New York, or Singapore, or any of hundreds of big towns all over the world. But they didn't have a Chamber of Commerce in those days to pipe down on the undesirable publicity; and when you stop to think that most of the high flyers in those little towns all packed guns, I think they did mighty well to keep the working hours of the Coroner within reasonable bounds.

Those towns always reminded me of beach resorts, for they were somnolent in Winter and wide-awake in Summer. During the hard winter months, with the freeze-up and severe prairie blizzards, there was little activity. Railroad building was slowed down to a drag; freighting was negligible; buffalo hunters were holed up and broke; the cattle trails were deserted; and there was not much for the town folks to do but sit around the hot stove and look forward to the coming thaw and the sucker season. But just let the white mantle disappear from the outdoors, and the range turn green, and the merry lads from the open spaces commence to drift in with coins jingling in the buckskin pokes. Then it was that the lid commenced to rattle and dance from the accumulated steam, till pop! Up it blew so high that it landed in the tall grass where no one could find it. Besides, who'd care to look for it?

Of course, not all the cowboys hitting town after the long drives took to the primrose path. There were those with a calmer outlook who could avoid the wild type of amusement, and you might even have found some "God fearing" boys and even psalm singers in an outfit. But, taken by and large, the majority looked forward to their crude fun, took it as they found it, and after they got their necks filled up with that frontier liquid dynamite, anything was liable to happen.

On first arriving into town, most of them hit for the tonsorial parlors to get slicked up, shorn, shaved, moustaches trimmed and curled, maybe beards set, hair oiled up and perfumed to high heaven in the most approved fashion. There were no safety razors in those days, and even at home, shaving was generally a Saturday night affair. There were few razors in a trail outfit, and when those boys hit town they looked like animated doormats, for, believe me, those cold water washings on the long trail were not the kind of operations a beauty operator would recommend as a skin preservative. They all really needed even the superficial ministrations of the frontier barber.

After the seance with the barber, some sorely needed shopping might be done, and the Jew merchant generally outfitted our wandering waddies with some pretty snappy hand-me-downs. Then, all slicked up, there was mighty little else to do but to get lickered up, gamble, or go see the girls. One had to be pretty strong-minded and determined to sit around at the General Merchandise Store for amusement after the first few hours.

They tell us there's nothing sure in this world but Death and Taxes. Well, there's something else just as sure, and that's Trouble. Any hombre trailing for trouble was always positively sure he'd find it. And that's what caused most of the fireworks in the old cowtowns. Boys out looking for fun, boys that were touchy, exuberantly independent and careless, they could very easily bump into trouble without looking for

it. But just let them commence to gargle the merry mucilage in copious drafts, and it was but a step into Old Man Trouble's trail. Especially, you must remember, as these lads packed shooting irons on their hips, all of which could easily lead to volcanic results.

So, all the more credit must be given to the waddies who kept away from the high rollings. The communities were small, and there were no public libraries, no movies, no Y.M.C.A., no Travelers' Aides with nice hostesses to give the home touch to the reception. Oh, yes, there were plenty of hostesses, all right, but it cost money and often plenty grief to play with them. Altogether, it was a hard set-up for the lonesome cowboy to side step.

There were plenty of young hot-heads who were fundamentally good who stubbed their toes, tangled with Trouble, shot their way clear, and had to take enforced vacations in the brush. In a lawless

39

country where six-guns thump the hip, and a man is his own judge, jury, and law enforcer, it's not a long span from a good enough boy who is decidedly independent and can brook no restraint, to the badman with a killer reputation. And when alcohol figured in the blend, it was but a step. Once a start was made on the crooked trail, it was mighty hard to turn off from the wild bunch of ladinos to the tame herd and the mansos. There was many a wild lad who survived the later cleanups of the law and order days to live and turn into a devout home body, a pillar of the church and society, yet who had to maintain a constant and tight clamp on the family closet door to keep the skeleton from rattling out and exposing the unlawful notches on the handle of the old hog leg.

II

mong the very early cowmen, the long hair was quite prevalent. This was not worn in a spirit of Wild West showmanship, as really happened in many cases later on after Buffalo Bill, Ned Buntline, and the lurid dime novels created a Wild West type for eastern consumption. In the ante bellum days, and those immediately following, the trend in masculine coiffure was for long hair. I do not mean that in all cases it had to drape over the shoulders, but it was for long locks. That was the natural trend in all branches of society, and so it was but natural that on the frontier where a man might go for months and months without even an approach to a barber shop, long-hairs were not an uncommon note. Moustaches were the vogue, and the smooth face was the exception; and that generally due to extreme youth or the inability to raise one. And let me state right here that there were some wonderful handlebars to be found in those days. Goatees were also quite popular, and, as a rule, cowboys looked older than they do today.

Although some of the old-timers might have worn linen "store boughten" shirts, you would never catch one with a "biled shirt" on; and it was quite general to find them with linsey-woolsey or hickory shirts. A little later, the flannel shirt came into great vogue, preferably the kind with the shield front and mother of pearl buttons around the border. Navy blue was the prevalent color, though fire-red ones were worn by a few leaning to the spectacular.

Southern men were much inclined to dark clothes, and the black pants, with stripes and even checks, were common. Overalls were unknown then as cowboy apparel. Galluses were seldom worn, and

JO MORA

*Early Texan
Cowman on his little
Spanish paint pony.*

pants were held in place by the snugness of the fit around the hips, or by a sash tightly bound. As a rule, pants legs were tucked into high boots. At that period, boots were quite the common footgear for men, even with well-dressed city folks, and many of the early trail herders wore that type. In fact, some of the very early ones wore the soft buckskin "half-breed" wrapped legging; and fringed pants and blouses of the same material were not unknown. Also, strange to say for a cowman, even moccasins were worn.

The "cowboy boot from Coffeyville" came in later, yet once it caught on, nothing else in the world could take its place with this rough and ready hombre, though you'd think it would have been just the opposite. The heels were high and narrow and often greatly underslung. The foot was of soft kid and fitted like a glove, and the tops were soft. They'll tell you that the high heels were made to keep the foot from slipping into and through a stirrup. Shucks, they may help in that respect, but I'd say they were invented to discourage a waddie from ever learning how to walk. I've stumped around in cowboy boots, on and off, all my life; and I'm now convinced they act on a man like dope, and once you acquire the habit, it's mighty hard to shake. One can get used to anything in this world, even the itch, so I'll confess I like them very much. Anyhow, whether you like them or not, they are as American as the Stars and Stripes, and their counterpart cannot be found anywhere else for a working man's footgear.

Cowboy boots were generally made of calfskin, fitting the lower leg snugly after the folded-over pants had been tucked inside. On some ranges, later on, pants were worn outside of the boot. Boot tops were high, and on many, the upper front half was a separate piece of colored calfskin, generally red or blue, with some design embroidered or stitched on . . . a lone star, a horseshoe, etc. I've seen some of the cheaper ones with these designs stamped on in gold or silver lacquer. Later this style was abandoned, and then the embellishments consisted only of scroll designs in rows of stitching: the more rows the greater the value. Now the modern boots run riot in the extravagance of their ornaments. They have inlays of all colors, fancy stitching, and even carved and stamped designs of flowers, bucking horses, steers, brands, initials, names, and anything the prospective owner may order. The bootstraps of canvas were generally allowed to stick up, and some of them had long "mule-ear" leather straps which dangled and flapped around on the outside. The soles were light, and the fit was snug around the foot, with the toe style varying from time to time. The tops were high and cut either straight across or curved on the sides. That was the old style boot, and with the passing of the old-timers, the moving picture heroes commenced designing what a cowboy should wear, and that's when they started getting fancier and fancier, and lower and lower till they got to the modern "peewee" which is quite worthless, in my opinion.

I'm just old-fashioned enough to still consider a cowboy as a working man and his boots according. Well, you can't tuck your pants into one of these contraptions because they just won't stay in; and you can't wear them outside because they won't stay out. They will catch on the edges and appear like they are trying hard to get back in, and altogether they look like hell.

Then again, have you ever been a flanker at a branding, "rasslin" calves? Well, if you have you know that you are sitting, or kneeling, or wiggling around on that dirty, dusty ground about as much as you are operating up on your hind legs; and if you're unlucky enough to be wearing a pair of those jokes, with tops about 8 or 9 inches high, you'll no doubt unhappily remember that every rock, pebble, and all the loose dirt within the radius of your activities (and a flanker is fairly active if the calves run big) hopped over and into the yawning maw. And if you're riding through the chaparral, your overalls are bound to work up over their tops, and it's mighty little brush you'll miss packing home with you inside those so-called boots. But the movie heroes and the rope

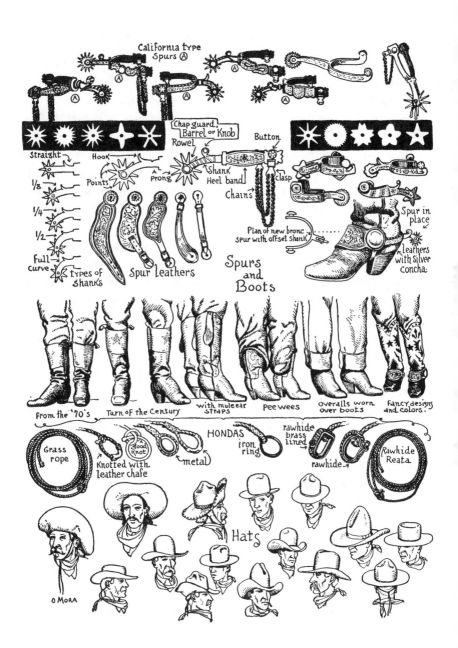

California type
Spurs Ⓐ

Chap guard, Barrel or Knob
Rowel

Button

straight
Hook
Points
Prong
Shank
Heel band
clasp
Chains

1/8
1/4
1/2
Full curve
types of shanks

Spur Leathers

Plan of new bronc spur with offset shank

Spurs and Boots

Spur in place

Leathers with Silver concha.

from the '70's
Turn of the Century
with muleear straps
pee wees
Overalls worn over boots
Fancy designs and colors.

Grass rope

Knotted with leather chafe

Good Knot

metal

HONDAS
iron ring

rawhide brass lined

rawhide

Rawhide Reata

Hats

O MORA

spinners at the Rodeo shows like them. I guess a lot of good top hands do too, or why do they wear them? I guess the trouble must be with me: that's the curse of getting old and out of tune with the times.

The old-time Texans wore heavy leather leggings to protect the hips and legs from the brush. The word "chaps" (pronounced "shaps") was not used then in the Lone Star State, though the Mexicans called theirs chaparreras or chaparejos. If he was a brush popper from the mesquitales of the Rio Bravo in southwest Texas, the chances are he'd be wearing a short, stout brushing jacket; otherwise he'd have an open vest, which was good for its pocket space.

In the evolution of the Cowboy there are four articles that were positively "standard equipment" with him, and some of them up to a fairly recent date, but which have either passed completely out of the picture or are seldom used now. These are the six-gun, the bandana or ample neck scarf, the gauntlet glove, and the quirt.

Let's take up first the six-gun. I think this little instrument has been the subject of more sensational bunk than anything else in the history of the "Wild West." Writers of so-called Western life have put over more slush on this subject than on any other phase. I'm not saying it did not play its tremendous role in the early life on the plains; far from it, for it did have a leading part. I'm only complaining of the magical, superhuman dexterity of its manipulation in general claimed by these experts.

When I was a boy, a cowboy was liable to catch cold if he sifted outdoors without a long-barreled hogleg chafing his hip as it swung in an open holster from a heavy, loosely buckled cartridge belt. Well, there's one thing to be said about packing a six-gun: it certainly showed up character in an individual, and made a young fellow feel plum full of importance and consequence. It showed one up as a reserved, not-to-be-trifled-with hombre, or a cocky, turbulent, dangerous pest. There was no half-way between stuff with gun toters. I have my own ideas on that subject, because I packed a gun myself in my youth, and also had occasion to see how it was used, and see how many could shoot, and how many couldn't. By and large, a goodly percentage of the cowboys that packed guns, and most of them did, would not have come into the money on the pistol range, in spite of your Wild West writers and movie heroes. Oh, I know this will raise a heck of an argument, but I still hold to my assertion. It is very true there were some who were "naturals" and clever with the revolver. There were also many high rollers and citizens of doubtful ambitions who took the time and had the perseverance to expert themselves in its use. They just had to, or else. . . . But these did not make up the vast majority, no more than they do today.

Most barroom brawls were quite deadly because the festivities generally took place within a range of from two to fifteen feet, and all they had to do was to point their artillery in the general direction and cut loose. In ranges from fifty feet up, believe me the bull's-eyes scored were no more prevalent than they are today. And if you don't believe it, go out and make your own investigations.

The boys packed their shooting-irons in open holsters in all kinds of weather, and, in time, they got so rusty and full of dirt and sand as to render them dangerous enough, but certainly no precision instruments. You must remember that the old-time cowboy worked out in the open all day, and generally slept out in the open all night, and was pretty dog-gone tired and careless when he rolled into his blanket. Cleaning outfits were not often at hand, and there was little inclination to use them had they been handy. All this did not make for the best kind of a set-up in the good care of firearms. Also, we had no non-corrosive primers in those days, and after a shot or two at a wolf or a coyote, long neglect and no cleaning, the inside of that barrel soon looked like the barnacled keel of a longshore wreck. Let me repeat that the foregoing remarks do not apply to *all* guns on the old frontier, but they do to a majority of them.

47

Your fiction or movie hero drags his artillery from the holster with a rapidity that baffles the eye, and opens up his salvos right from the hip, ringing bull's-eyes one, two, three! Just like that! And if he doesn't want to kill his opponent he just lops off his trigger finger, though said opponent be as full of action as a flea on a hot griddle. Muchacho! Those hombres are sho nuf poison with the flying lead.

I guess I haven't been around much because I never did see any of those real gun artists out in the open. I don't say they didn't exist: I just say that I never saw them. I have seen and known quite a few crack shots with the six-gun, in my life, but I guess they would not count because most of them always tried to take as careful an aim as time and the exigency of the situation allowed them. And another wizard I've never seen in action is the famous one that holds back his trigger and fans the hammer with the palm of his other hand, tapping the gong at every rapid fan. So, I'll confess, I haven't seen everything, except, of course, in the movies.

Anyhow, the old-time cowboy and his shooting iron were inseparable, whether he was a dead shot or not, or just packed it about as a social obligation if not a necessity. Gunpowder and alcohol make a nasty blend, and it soon got so that the boys were asked to check their hardware when they drifted into the thirst emporiums to attend to their serious drinking. Later on they were even asked to check those toys on entering certain unromantic towns. At last, however, the forces of law and order got pretty well organized, and it wasn't long before some States and Territories passed laws prohibiting the carrying of concealed weapons, and some even those that were not concealed.

So it came that one picturesque phase of the early West passed out. There were many die-hards of the old regime, though most people welcomed the change. Of course, the bad little boys packed them just the same, concealed, law or no law, exactly as it is done today. But Man gets accustomed to anything pretty pronto, and the days of the gun-toting cowboy passed into history. There is no denying that the ready gun of the open holster had been a potent factor in the opening up of cattleland, and quite responsible for many a change in the status quo. However, in offense and defense, the gun toters had to think fast and act faster, for to reach for it hesitatingly or bluff at it, was simply courting suicide. Yes, many a brave lad stayed to grow up with the country because he was dilatory in playing with that dangerous toy.

Every type of revolver, pistol, and derringer of the period was to be found on the old frontier, but a certain type soon established itself as the popular one in cowboy circles. That was the long-barreled, heavy, solid frame, single action revolver. The first were, of course, the cylinder loading, percussion cap type. The best of these were Remingtons and Colts; and what well-balanced weapons most of them were! When cartridges came into use, the .41, .44 and .45 were the popular calibers, and the single action retained its popularity even after the double usurped the field. Five of the six cylinders were generally loaded, and the hammer let down on the empty chamber.

To facilitate the draw, and so that the holster would not stick to the gun if the fit was snug, the tip end of the holster was tied to the leg with the two long thongs that dangled there. This could not be done over wing chaps. Anyhow, the belts were worn rather loose, and the heavy gun in its holster hung free and pounded a tatoo on the hip of the rider or the cantle of the saddle when the pony loped. I have seen bronc twisters, plenty of them, forked on a wildly weaving hurricane deck, while that heavy gun wove as wildly at every jump, the loose belt at times climbing almost to the rider's arm-pits. And I've seen guns go flying out of those holsters like rockets, too, under such conditions. Why we packed guns on jobs of that kind and in that way, is a mystery to me now, though it seemed perfectly natural then. We often tied the gun into the holster with a loose piece of whang strung through a hole at the top. Of course, it was freed when the owner drifted into a hostile zone or one that had the earmarks of turning into such. Ah, them was the days!

Next in order comes the bandana, or scarf around the neck, which seems to have passed out. Except for some of the boys and girls in the Rodeo parades, you don't see them often on working cowboys any more. In the old days, however, a waddie felt embarrassed and undressed if caught out in society without his bandana. Generally it ran to reds in color, though neck pieces went the full gamut of the palette from white to blue and black, and made of silk, or cotton, or linen. The knotted ends were worn at the back, and if not placed that way, they generally worked around to that position anyhow. The uses to which this bit of haberdashery was put, seemed limitless, and to try enumerating them would be to go through the entire daily routine of the wandering cowhand. However, here's a few: as a towel, personal or dish; bronc blind; tourniquet; pigging string; sling; water filter; ear muff; hot handle pad; and one of the most popular uses was to tighten it over the bridge of the nose and let the folds hang loosely over the mouth to act as a filter in the choking dust of a cattle column. Then, too, this same position was considered very fashionable by the brave lads who took to the crooked trails and used it as an efficient mask to hide their identities.

Anyhow, the good old bandana seems to have passed out in the march of progress. Now, the bowlegged boys can shed their ponies and climb aboard a benzine buggy that will snake them pronto to where they can get in touch with the many accessories for which the old bandana substituted, even if crudely at times. However, it had its place, it seen its duty and it done it. I still like to wear one when I go into the hills on a pack trip.

Another article of cowboy wearing apparel that has passed out to join the dodo in his hermitage, is the fringed, buckskin gauntlet of past days. Originally the Cowboy was a gloved knight, and in his daily routine of riding, roping, branding, etc., the flying fringes of his gauntlets

50

gave an accent to his costume that was mighty picturesque and distinctive. These were, as a rule, made of fine buckskin, and the ample cuffs were often embroidered or stitched with fancy designs. The star was the most popular motive, especially with the boys from the Lone Star State. This could be embroidered with colored silk or with silver thread. Horseshoes, and horse heads, and flowers were also popular. Then, too, I have seen a few real cowboys (no, not squaw men or breeds) wearing them with Indian beadwork. When a waddie peeled his gloves off, he generally stacked them, folded them over, and draped them on his cartridge or chap belt. But I guess you'd be pegged for a dude or a Hollywood boy if you blossomed out with fringed, embroidered gauntlets these days on what's left of the cow ranges.

Then there's that other article of former extreme popularity, the Quirt. You'll seldom see one in use these days, and yet there was a time when the cowpuncher and his quirt were about as inseparable as the cowpuncher and his spurs. Yes, it seems that the old-time quirt is slowly wiggling its way into the museum cabinet of past range history. I can't exactly figure the reason for this, as I firmly believe that in the early handling of broncs and in the later period of teaching them to rein and be real cowponies, the quirt, in the hands of one who really savvies its use, is an aid that is priceless.

The quirt was made of plaited leather or rawhide, with either a flexible shank or one built on an iron rod or wooden core. A Turk's Head was generally at the top, with a loop of whang strung in a hole passing through it, or leading out from the core through the top of the head. There might be several other knots in the shank, and always a couple of snappers about a foot long. Designs varied a bit, and also many were loaded, making them easier to swing and likewise to use as a blackjack of no mean possibility. Horsehair quirts were also made, but the real working tool was of leather or rawhide. Your old-timer did not loop his over the wrist and grasp the handle with his hand when he wanted real results, but ran his first two fingers through the loop and let it swing from a flexible pivot. Boy! Could he raise the welts and make his critter get a wiggle on himself!

Some of the boys just looped it over the horn when not in use, but a much better gadget for packing it was from a snap at the rear rosette of the offside jockey. It was handy, easy to reach, and still out of the way. No one wanted a quirt dangling from the wrist while roping, and if on the horn it certainly wasn't the best place when the dallies smoked at the snubbing. It didn't make so much difference with the hard and fast boys.

Although you could scarcely call any of the cowboy's working tools "foreign," yet there is one which is American and American only. That one is his flying loop, call it by any one of its many names . . . lazo, lasso, lasoo, lass rope, rope, string, reata, lariat, etc. This tool falls into two categories: one made of rawhide, the other of fibre. The latter may be of Manila hemp, Mexican maguey, sisal, linen or cotton. The last two better suited for rope spinners and showmen than for working men on the ranges. However, all kinds have a slip knot or other device at one end with which to make a running noose. This is called the honda, hondo or hondoú. It all comes from the Spanish honda, which is pronounced without the "h." This may be of rawhide, old California style, in a couple of slightly varying types; or it can be of brass or galvanized iron, egg-shaped with concave body to fit inside the rope spliced over it; or it may be a metal ring; or one of several metal devices which act as chafes; or the end may be knotted into a bowline loop with or without a leather or rawhide chafe stitched on. Lasso, lasoo, lass rope are English derivatives from the Spanish lazo. Reata is straight Spanish; and lariat is the English corruption of "la reata" (the reata). Reatas are always made of rawhide, although a lariat may be either rawhide or grass. The word "string" is used for either one, though to definitely specify the rawhide article, "skin string" is sometimes used.

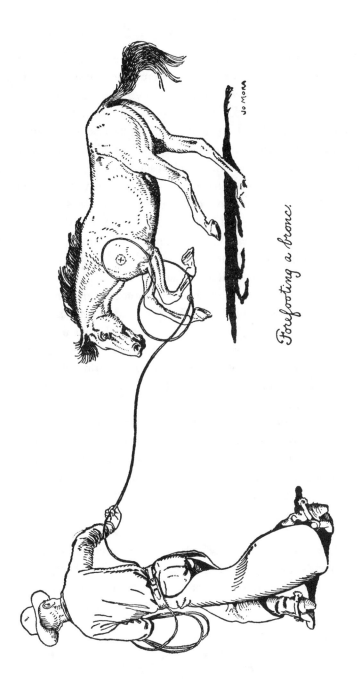

Forefooting a bronc.

The rawhide reata was the original article, and throughout the Spanish and Mexican cow country, reateros grew up that were masters at the craft of braiding reatas and all other vaquero rawhide tools, many of which were truly works of art. In our own country, California was where the making of reatas reached its highest peak. At the time of the first World War, with the scarcity of rawhide, aided and abetted by the modern methods of working stock in small corrals, chutes, and whatnots, the art seemed to be petering out and there was a dearth of good reateros. But things seem to work in cycles, and with the renaissance of popularity for the stock horse and the western rig, there are now a few modern reateros who can hold their own with any of the past. They are real masters of the craft, and believe me it takes masters to turn out some of these rawhide masterpieces.

The finest reatas are made from the primest parts only of several young heifer hides, well chosen, properly cured, and the strands cut by an expert. The braiding must also be done with that uniformity and even tension that only your true reatero knows. In the old days, most of the boys tried to do their own rawhide work during idle winter days in outlying cow camps. Some fair jobs resulted, too; and then again, what a crop of lumpy, kinky, cockeyed, would-be reatas have I seen as the result of those lonesome winter days. I tried it myself.

A good rawhide braider of cowboy tools should not only be a master craftsman, but he should also be a good stockman and know the game thoroughly. Then his goods will reflect that knowledge, and if he makes improvements he knows why he does it from actual experience. The making of fine reatas seems to run in families, and here in California, from the very early days of the Dons, one prominent example is the name of Ortega. This is almost synonymous with good rawhide work. Forty years ago I bought a couple of fine Ortega reatas, one new, the other used and supposed to be quite old. You may still buy, or have custom made today, as finely braided and beautifully balanced reatas of the same name, as at any time in the old heyday of the California vaquero. Well, I hope the reata never goes out of the picture while cows are cows and men work them from the backs of ponies.

There are two systems used in roping, one with a short string of 30 or 40 feet, one end tied fast to the saddle horn. This is called the "hard and fast" way. The other is with a longer string, unattached, the operator taking his turns around the horn and holding on to the string to snub. This is called the "dally" way. The word dally comes from the Spanish "dale" (dáh-leh) and it's what the Gringo coined from hearing the Vaqueros call out to the ropers, "Dale vuelta! Dale vuelta!" (Give it a turn! Give it a turn!) In true Yankee brevity, however, the "dale" alone was retained—we spell it dally, though it only means "Give it," and they let "vuelta" drift, though that's what really meant "the turn." The hard and fast boys use the grass rope; the dally boys use both.

Reatas are braided in 4, 6, or 8 strands. The latter two, especially the 8, if made by a top reatero, is a beautiful article and superb for light roping. For the average hard work on large stock, the 4-strand is the best. Diameters vary according to individual preference, but the ⅜-inch reata is the one most used. Naturally, a hand-made reata costs considerably more than a grass rope, yet, though it is vulnerable to certain accidents, with proper care and luck it should outlast a half dozen grass ones.

All new ropes, grass or rawhide, should be stretched properly to get them in good working shape. A grass rope is often stretched from post to post, one end tied to an extra rope, or better a chain, and this is twisted with a stick or a bar to shorten it up to the desired tautness and left overnight. A reata is generally tied to a post and a couple of turns taken on the horn with a quiet horse that will walk off slowly. The dallies are allowed to slip along with a good tension which warms up and stretches the reata. If this has been neglected and allowed to dry up and get out of shape, this is a fine way to bring it back, with a good stretching and an application of tallow. The heat of the slipping dallies and the opening up of the pores in the hide with the stretching, takes the tallow in fine shape. Saddle soap is a good dressing, but mineral oils should be avoided.

The laws of supply and demand and the matter of economy was what first gave the grass rope its popularity. Modern trends for more speed and less time for leisure, a laziness and more often an inability to braid their own gear, and the grass rope came into the picture to stay. A waddie could stump into the trading post or general merchandise emporium and buy him 30 or 40 feet of whale line from a big coil at a small cost and whenever he wanted it. Then, too, ropes were also made up with hondas for ready sale, many of them passing through the mail order houses and ultimately to the ranges. I've used both rawhide and grass, and I've seen them used for many years, and to classify them broadly, I would say that the grass rope was the efficient tool of the rough and ready, "let's go" operator: and the reata that of the finished artist, a sensitive, elastic, vibrant gear.

In former years, the reata was the popular gear on the Pacific Coast, in Nevada, and parts of Arizona and New Mexico. The Spanish and Mexican vaqueros of California were the first of the breed of dally boys in the United States, and it was here they reached their spectacular peak with the long reata . . . la reata larga. In Texas and on the Great Plains, the cowboys rode right on top of their critters to spill the small loop of their thirty-foot whale line where it would do the most good . . . right around the horns. Then they jerked up the slack, flipped the rope over to the off side of the critter, and swung their racing pony away to near side. The other end of that line was tied hard and fast to the saddle horn and the case went to the jury pronto without any arguments.

The dally boy, chances are, packed a 65- to 85-foot reata, shook out a very big loop, and, if he was good, could make his cast even 50 or 60 feet away. Now, brother, jamming the breeze wide open after spooky

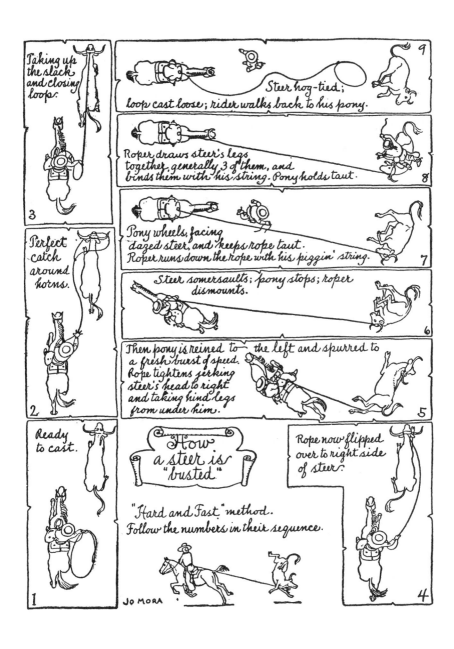

Taking up the slack and closing loop.

3

Perfect catch around horns.

2

Ready to cast.

1

Steer hog-tied; loop cast loose; rider walks back to his pony.

9

Roper draws steer's legs together, generally 3 of them, and binds them with his string. Pony holds taut.

8

Pony wheels, facing dazed steer, and keeps rope taut. Roper runs down the rope with his piggin' string.

7

Steer somersaults; pony stops; roper dismounts.

6

Then pony is reined to the left and spurred to a fresh burst of speed. Rope tightens jerking steer's head to right and taking hind legs from under him.

5

How a steer is "busted"

Rope now flipped over to right side of steer.

"Hard and Fast" method. Follow the numbers in their sequence.

JO MORA

4

stock, this is no chore for a ploughman. I'm not saying one system is better than the other. I've used both, I respect both, and I only wish I had been better at them than I am. It just depends on what the job is that's got to be done. The hard and fast for rough and ready speed; the dally for the artist. In flat, open country the former is tops; but take it in the rough hills with lots of scattered trees and patches of chapparal, the long reata and the dally system, in the hands of an expert, are unbeatable. He'll play his critter like a fisherman with a trout, and he'll weave in and out of dangerous hazards and pick his spot for the snub. And if the showdown pops up where it would really pay dividends to cast loose from even a $30.00 reata, he can do it in a split second.

And yet, it seems to me, we're training less and less dally boys every year. The modern Rodeo show has a great influence on Cowboy ways, because it's there the big money can be found by the boy who has got what it takes. And don't kid yourself that the boys on the back ranges don't dream of some day cashing in to the roar of the big grandstands. Of course there's just one goal there for roping, and that is SPEED, SPEED, SPEED. Barring the team roping event, which is not on all programs, the other calls only for hard and fast operation, and you can bet the boys are going to concentrate and practise on that only, The arena grounds are kept up and as flat as a table, and what is needed is a flash pony, a short line and a short cast.

Breastplates are now being used with the roping rigs, and cantles are getting lower and lower, with some as flat as an English saddle seat. In vaulting out of the saddle, to make the tie, the leg might pass over that low cantle in a fraction of a second less: and one must admit that might mean just the difference between getting into the money or kissing the entry fee good-bye. However, there's no argument about the fact that we are rapidly drifting from real range cow work to circus showmanship. Nothing wrong with it, I might say; just the trend of human events and the great evolution going on and on. Maybe all this

The reata larga muchachos spread a mighty big loop in their long distance operations.

JO MORA

helps to perpetuate the type, and some day in the dim, dim future, when the ranges are all settled up with housing problems and the human animal has been broken to eat synthetic beef, our circus cowboy will still be entertaining the grandstands. He'll be riding robot ponies and roping mechanical dogies in nothing flat; and he'll also be keeping alive the memories of when his ancestral cowboy was first born and operated as a distinct American type to act as nurse to real beef for the world to eat.

With the hard and fast type of roping coming into greater popu-

59

larity, the flank cinch is gradually creeping into the picture more and more, and we find it edging into the old, dyed-in-the-wool single rig ranges. When I first drifted into California, over forty years ago, it was almost a felony, on the statute books, for a vaquero to be seen in public forking a double rig. But them days have gone forever, and the flank cinch, or at least the ring for same, has come to stay, and you'll find it on 50 per cent of the new custom-built California saddles. It won't be long now. And that's how evolutions come; and I've seen plenty in Cowland, in my time.

The old-time California vaquero, the master of "la reata larga," was not out for speed records, and did not follow the professional Rodeo shows for the obvious reason that there were no such things in his day, while there was a heap too much of "mañana" in his veins to worry over just what fraction of a second he could cut off this or cut off that. But he did fuss and put in a lot of time working up and practising fancy throws and catches.

I really hesitate at times to write about some of the tricky roping I've seen done by some of those old-timers. Their pride was a big loop, a long, long throw, and all sorts of seemingly impossible catches. Not accidental ones, but called in advance. Figure 8's from the saddle, on unhazed, running wild stock, were quite ordinary and not the exception. The "piale" was a throw tossed underhand right back of the front legs under the belly of the running quarry, the loop opening up so that the hind legs stepped into it. The "mangana" was an overhand flip, the loop opening in front for the forefeet to step into. Another pretty throw and a grand one to bust a critter high, wide and handsome, was the one that was cast over the off shoulder of the running critter, the loop whipping around and opening up to snare the forefeet. And make no mistake about this one not spelling "buenas noches" when the dallies were taken and the pony's tail set to the ground.

There were so many different throws, and each one had its own

1 **a tricky throw** — a powerful side-arm throw. big standing loop circles steer from behind.

2 Loop travels forward fast.

3 Lower part of loop hits back of steer's front legs. the top tipping over and clearing steer's head.

4 Roper quickly closes loop.

5 Roper takes his dallies; pony squats; steer somersaults.

6 and that's all, folks!

JO MORA

name. Yet, of all the intricate throws I have ever seen on the range with wild stock, there was one which I first saw done twice in succession on a bet, and have never seen completed again since that day over forty years ago. I have seen it attempted several times, and by top ropers, but never completed. It's a throw where the big loop, standing up, sneaks right up from behind, clears the hind legs when they are off the ground, encircles the animal and keeps traveling forward with the upper part clearing the back and head till the lower part of the loop hits the back of the front legs causing the top to whip down and is then jerked tight around the front legs. It's a very difficult and tricky throw, especially from horseback on the dead run. The big loop must be thrown with a powerful delivery to travel fast, wide open and standing up, with the lower part just shaving the ground and no more. That's where the tricky part and the element of luck comes in, for it's big odds against the roper no matter how well executed the throw has been. The lower part of the loop *must clear* those hind feet just when they are both off the ground. The sketch I've made of it will readily show this throw clearer than my possibly confusing description.

As I stated before, I saw this done twice in succession on a sidehill overlooking the Santa Ynez River in California, a few miles from what is now the town of Solvang. This was at the turn of the century, and nobody ever thought of a town there then. Only the old Mission drowsed in the sunshine, and the little, old Donohue ranch buildings sprawled near the river bottom. I was new to California then, and though I had heard some tall stories of those reata larga vaqueros, I had never seen one of these skin-string top hands operate. I had been riding in Texas, double cinch and a short grass rope, and I had seen and known a lot of sureshot ropers. Also I had known many A-1, tip-top ropers in old Mexico from the Rio Grande to Tierra Caliente; real artists with the dally rope, maguey or rawhide. So, as I always try to steer clear of the smart hombre who is forever telling that this or that is the *best* in the world, I'll just state that when I saw that paisano juggle his reata larga (and it was all of that, 85 feet of it) I knew that I had drifted into the company of a real Cowboy, and one who savvied what it was all about. I knew a grand crop of dally men in California in those days. They were none of them boys. In fact, most were past middle age, and a few had been taking their dallies before the Gringo took over. They were the tag end of the real old Spanish-California school.

One of the questions I'm often asked is about the length of the average reata, and how far can a catch be made. The first is easy to answer; the second not so easy. Ropes vary in length according to the individual taste or ability of the user. I'd say that a 45-foot reata was a short one, and 65 feet a long average. However, the old-timers packed reatas that were *much longer.* I have seen and measured two that went over 100 feet. One of them, 105 feet by yardstick measurement; the other a trifle over 109 feet by my own "brasada" measurement, and in those days I could hit it mighty close. A brasada measure is the length a man can stretch out his arms holding a reata. That's the way reatas were bought in those days: it paid to have a boarding house reach then. Now I call those two samples I've just mentioned, Reatas Largas in any man's vocabulary. Unless you're a roper and have worked with one of these long toys, you can't imagine what kind of a handful those vaqueros had to juggle. If you ever get hold of one, just try it. It will prove itself better than any words I can write about it. It's not only holding that big coil in your fist along with the reins, but it's the controlling of it: letting out the coils or taking them back as the play may demand. If you don't think it's the biggest and trickiest handful you ever had when in action, well, you're a better man than I am and think differently. Though let me say right here that I never was a "natural" with the long reata. I just got by, and not so hot at that.

Examine the tail end of your reata and notice the way it is finished.

It will not take much of your imagination to see why they call that the cascabel. "Cascabel" is the Spanish word for a certain kind of bell, a jingle-bob, the *rattle of the rattlesnake*. It is this last mentioned that I refer to here. Some of the old-time vaqueros often took a couple of dallies on the horn at the last couple of feet of their reatas and led the loose end with the cascabel under the right leg to be held by pressure against the saddle. One had to ride close, because if he loosened or wove around too much, he'd stand to lose his dallies. This trick was really the original starter of the hard and fast system. I have not seen this done for many, many years in California, though it was quite the stunt in the old reata larga days. And another thing that's also passed out, is the weighting of the reatas with shot. This was done for those abnormally long throws in windy weather.

To answer the question of how far a catch can be made, I'll state that there's no easier way to start an insurrection among ropers than to begin giving extreme statistics in this matter. I have heard of many throws that would be startling records, and really I have every reason to believe they are true, but I'm going to forego all that, and just state what I have seen myself time and again under working conditions, and not trick stuff. I've seen plenty of catches at the full length of an 85-foot reata, which, allowing for the big loop and the wobble in the coils, would be about 60 feet, more or less. And that, Buddy, is a long, long ways from home.

And speaking of insurrections, here's another recipe for starting one. Just part out a couple of grass rope, hard and fast fanatics, and haze them into the cut with an equal number of reata-dally zealots. Then start the argument and it won't be long for the fireworks. One will claim that a pesky rawhide reata kinks so that you can't make it lie flat or build a fast loop with it that will stay open. Then will come a counter that you've got to take your new grass rope to bed with you in cold, damp weather or else go find a coil of wire for something soft enough

to rope with, while on days when old Sol really does get to work, the danged thing goes as limp as a dishrag and you couldn't throw a loop with it against a sneeze. And so the battle will rage, both sides right and both sides wrong. And you can start the same kind of a battle over the merits of single versus the double rig; or the half-breed port versus the Spanish spade; or the snaffle versus the hackamore for breaking broncs. These hot air encounters have been going on since the cow-game was first organized in this country, and they'll keep up till old Gabe drags out the bugle and gathers up all the cow waddies for the last big round-up. Even then I doubt if the discipline will be stiff enough to snub the arguments.

Dudes, yes and even some pretty fair grass ropers, when they first handle a new, well-made reata, find it is something they know little about. I've heard them complain that a reata kinks too easy, and that you can't make it lie flat; and that the loop snarls and closes too easily, etc., etc. Well, that's all true enough, but it's the fault of the operator, not the reata. A good new one is an elastic, willowy, you might almost say "live" tool. It has a natural tendency to coil one way. The truth is that it's more than a tendency: it will coil one way and one way only. And that's the way you've got to handle it or else quit trying to play with it. Never start coiling from the honda. Always start from the casca-bel end, and as you lay your coils, you'll feel it resist and start to kink. At that point give it a flip and a twist with the hand till you feel it "relax" and then lay your coil. Just keep repeating this and you'll coil it up in just one way and it'll lie as flat as it should. But don't try to fool it or force it in place in any other way. It will tell YOU all about it, and if you are inexperienced or bull-headed about it, you'll wind up with a handful of kinks that will make you either laugh or cuss. Do you wonder I say the damned thing feels like it's alive? The same thing applies when you let out the coils to build your loop. You just feed the coils through your honda with a reverse twist to turn the rope.

66

And while we're on the subject of rawhide cowboy tools, let's take up the Hackamore. That, from my experience and observations, is the most misunderstood and seldom properly used implement. And this applies not alone to dudes, but likewise to many a so-called horse breaker among the professionals and stockmen. I'm continually asked by the uninitiated what magic that funny looking halter possesses that will break and rein a colt: and also how can a wild colt be controlled without a bit? And that's where the trouble lies. Too many, even among those who should know better, seem to think there is some magic to it, and that once it's fastened on a bronc's features, all the breaker has to do is to sit tight and watch an ornery hunk of bronco turn into a well-behaved and flash-reined cowpony.

These remarks are not made with a desire to wisecrack; they are just from a reaction after watching some modern horsebreakers (who get paid for their efforts, too) trying to break and rein their colts with hackamores when they don't understand the basic principal of it. I've seen the bosals on some hackamores so cluttered with gadgets of torture on them that they looked like the pipe dreams of a Rube Goldberg: sticks, wedges, wires, bolts, bones, and what-nots.

But first, take a look at the sketch of a hackamore and see what a simple tool it is. It's just composed of a braided rawhide bosal (nose band) with two strips of latigo whang interlaced to either side to act as cheek-plates and tie at the poll to hold it in place. That's all there generally is to them. Buckles are seldom used. Some may have a browband of the same narrow whang, or a throat latch. There are some amansadores (tamers) who rig a leather or rawhide band which slides up and down the cheek pieces, and is used as a blind (tapa-ojos). They slide it down and cover the colt's eyes with it for saddling or mounting, and they can lift it from the saddle and it keeps its place above the eyes then like a wide browband. If you'll look at the sketch, you'll notice how close to the eyes the cheek strips come as they lead down and hook up

67

very high on the bosal at the two extremes of the nose button. This is so as to give more length and flexibility to the shanks when they are weighted down with the mecáte knot and reins. This should hang down well to properly clear the chin. The bosal has an extra braiding over the top part, tapering from the centre to the sides, and this is called the nose button. The shanks lead down and join in a heavy heel knot. There are a few slight variations in hackamores, some having double shanks with the ends meeting in a slip loop and button. But the first mentioned is the real old California jaquima (háh-kee-mah).

The reins for a hackamore are made up from a horse-hair rope called a mecáte (meh-cáh-teh). On certain ranges this is called a McCarthy, and it's plain to see how the Gringo derived it. These are made of horse-hair mane or tail (the former are the softest and best), mohair (very silky), and cowtail (very stiff and prickly). They average about 22 feet in length and have a tassel (la mota) at one end. They may be of one color hair, though generally they are of various colors, white, black, brown, sorrel, and many of them are very attractive.

To make up the reins you pass the tassel end through the shanks of the bosal over the heel knot and let it hang a few inches only. Lead the rope back and over at about the middle of the horse's back, looping it back again on the other side to the heel knot where you give it several wraps and make up one of a few different knots. The long loose end is pulled through these wraps and the knot tightened up, and the free part of the rope now serves as a lead or tie rope, averaging about 12 or 14 feet in length. The tassel now hangs down jauntily and looks right smart on a well-tied knot. When a Twister eases himself onto the hurricane deck, he can coil this rope up and tie it to the saddle string at the fork, or he can tuck it under and over his belt; and if the going gets too rough for him and he's loosened for a spill, he can still grab that mecate and wind up with a handful of bronco, anyhow.

A plain hackamore, with the bosal properly balanced to the indi-

A California buckaroo.

vidual colt's head, the mecate knot well adjusted so that the heel knot and side shanks hang nicely to clear the under jaw at the chin, should be sufficient for a good man in the saddle with light hands at the reins to educate the average colt. However, bear in mind that there's always the exception to every rule. We might agree that to educate and instruct a person the best way is by fairness and kindness: yet that does not mean that every now and then a poor, cockeyed lunatic won't show up that forces the use of a padded cell and a strait-jacket. Well, it's the same with the plain hackamore. Every now and then you'll catch up with a bronc that's thick-skinned, tough in fibre, and heedless of pain. It's then the good hackamore operator may add a little roughening to his side bars, a binding of hard-laid cord, or a small bone fastened with rawhide. But these should be considered only temporary necessities for a short time at the start. Often, on tough-hided specimens, we use the rougher cow-hair reins. Anyhow, the secret, if you want to call it that, is to get the bosal that fits the bronc, with the proper hang to the heel and rein knot so that when the reins are loose it will clear the jaw by an inch and a half, more or less according to the conformation of the muzzle or the temperamental requirements of the animal.

Naturally, a wild colt will resent strenuously every move on that first day, and he's bound to get roughed and rawed up a bit, especially at the chin. He's getting a tough, hard lesson, which is as it should be, but don't rub it in too much on the second day. Unless your colt is one of those thick-skinned or criminal specimens, and you'll find them plenty in the horse world, you should ease up on that tender spot at the chin and ride with as gentle a hand as possible. This is no "cruelty to animals" sermon, it's cold, hard facts to the secret of breaking a colt to be a gentle, well reined animal. Give him half a chance and the colt will soon learn that if he holds his head down and at the proper angle he can keep things from aggravating that tender spot. That is, of course, if the hombre in the saddle helps by giving a loose rein. Show me the

Cheeking a bronc.

JO MORA

twister that rides with a tight rein, and I'll show you the one that will *not* turn out a sweet-mouthed cowpony.

However, just remember that putting flash reins on cowponies does not belong to the era of punching time clocks and speed productions. That's why such sweet-reined stock horses were found in California in the old days before the Gringo. Those amansadores had lots of savvy, plenty of patience, heaps of mañana, and a small value on time. There was the fountain head and home of the jaquima in these United States of ours. A colt would be worked six months or a year with a hackamore; then he'd be made to pack a bit for a while extra without any reins attached to it; and then he'd graduate into the two-reined

71

class, which was to use both the hackamore and mecate, and the spade bit and reins. That is where he'd get his thorough and final schooling. When, at last, that hackamore was discarded, the good average colt was a well-reined, sweet-mouthed stock pony that could spin on a two-bit piece with a loose rein, back straight with slight pressure, and from high speed set the roots of his tail to the weeds and slide to a stop with those hind legs tucked beautifully under him.

The hackamore trainer just fools that colt into thinking there's some kind of a potent hokus-pokus to a bosal that can control him, and that's all there is to it. It's just a mental flimflam. But don't go continually "leaning on the reins" for he'll then learn differently and you'll have to begin adding those cockeyed gadgets I referred to, and you'll have to keep on hurting him more and more as he hardens to them. And that is *not* the hackamore method.

After the first day's natural roughing around and rawing up a bit, the good trainer pulls up to remind that colt he's got a tender spot under the chin only when he needs correction; then eases up at once. Otherwise it's to be avoided and that knot must drop down and away from the tender spot. When he's taught to turn, the rider should bring his head around with a down pull; steady and hard if necessary, but always down to keep that knot away from the sensitive spot as much as possible. Then a loose rein at once when the lesson is finished. A clever hackamore amansador can just work wonders with a colt in time. But it takes time and plenty of it, and adjustments may have to be made to the hackamore as the education proceeds. Often different hackamores are used. Plenty of savvy, plenty of patience, plenty of mañana: that's what it takes.

Well, the fame of this system got wafted to ranges where colts were always broken with a bit right from the start, and it seemed that everybody who had a colt to break and rein started using hackamores. Some found out what it was all about and got fine results; yet there were plenty of bullheads who took it up just to prove to the outside world that the derned thing wouldn't work so hot after all. Naturally it didn't. Then some thought the idea wasn't so bad, only it needed improvement. So they started to improve, and now there are several devices on the market of metal and with the leverage system but no bar in the mouth. I've never used one because the plain old hackamore is good enough for me, and so I can't argue pro or con on them.

What I can say, however, is that I see plenty of these lads with their hackamore broncs, and a big percentage of them might just as well be using halters or a rope half-hitched around the muzzle tightly. Many breeze around with that chin spot raw and bloody all the time; and lots of them, as I mentioned before, with all those torture gadgets hooked on to keep that spot forever sensitive and sore. Then again, some think that the bosal should be kept tight to control the colt, so, when horse-hair reins raw up the chin, they still keep it tight but add a piece of sheepskin for a chafe. These operators work on the theory that if you hurt a colt and keep him in continual pain you can handle him easier. In lots of cases the raw spots get calloused, and then you'll need more and more to get a reaction, like a Chink taking hop. And that's where all that junk comes in to keep it sensitive. Well, it may be just the opposite from the real hackamore theory, but it is a grand system to get a crop of jumpy, heady, nervous, touchy sky snifters and switch-tails. And the ranges are full of them: just go out and look 'em over, if you don't believe me.

The hackamore is sometimes used with a Fiador (fée-ah-dor), or, as many Americans called it, Theodore. This is made up with a small-diameter hair rope, or one of rawhide, or of white cotton sash cord. In a broad sense it acts as a throat-latch and converts the hackamore into a strong halter, as it goes around the neck and leads down under the jaws to tie into the bosal at the heel knot. The cord leads double all around, and the knots used in the ties are very tricky and smart looking. You may follow its construction better by studying the drawings of it than by any word description.

In the true hackamore, the bosal is supported by light cheek-plates, very often without even a browband or a throat latch, and though it will stand all kinds of pulling from a position in the saddle, from one in front, much pulling would likely jerk the bosal off the muzzle as all the strain would come on the two very light cheek-plates. So, when a Peeler dismounts from a hackamore bronc and wants to tie him up, he makes a clever hitch with the mecate reins around the colt's neck, draws them down tight to the bosal heel knot, and can then tie with the lead rope as safely as with a halter. But a hackamore with fiador is as solid as a halter all the time, and, if well tied, I think looks very snappy. The only objection I have to it is that it takes much of the flexibility out of the bosal and makes it too rigid and interferes with its proper hang. To my notion it is much better on advanced colts than green ones getting those all-important early lessons that make or break them.

I learned the use of the hackamore from amansadores of the old California school, and I think I understand and fully appreciate the "delicate sensitivity" of this tool, and I hate to see anything interfere with it. I knew one of those old paisanos that was snapping and reining broncs when, I'll bet, he was 45 or 50. He would make two or three alterations in the hang of his bosal during the first couple of weeks of breaking a bronc, and he'd often change hackamores two or three times more before the colt was finished. He'd explain to me why he made these changes, and I sure learned about broncos from him. Sometimes it was to get certain reactions from the physical conformation of the horse and sometimes it was to meet certain *temperamental* qualities. Now that may sound far-fetched to some readers, but that old boy certainly knew his horseflesh and it was all in the day's work with him. When he'd change he would always say to me, "No son todos los mismos" (they are not all the same). Anyhow, if you don't think that old boy knew the answers, you should have ridden some of the colts he broke. Oh, well, there's plenty will agree with me in what I've just aired up, and there's plenty, too, will give me the razz. But I expect that, and also know that those that do the snorting don't know what a hackamore is anyhow, even though they may think they do.

And while on the subject of reining, it's natural to drift right on to the subject of Bits. And there's another one of those Cowboy subjects that's plum full of dynamite wherever waddies of the different schools congregate. Those two schools are made up of the advocates of the Half-breed port Curb Bit, and those of the Spanish Spade Bit. Everything these days, even in Cowland, is heading more and more towards standardization. Time was, however, when, in a broad sense, you could draw a line down the Rockies, and, with few exceptions, call those west of it the Spade Bit School, and those east of it the Curb Bit School. The eastern boys, in Texas and the Great Plains, were inclined to break their broncs with a bit in the mouth, maybe a snaffle or low curb, right from the first jump. Later they rode their broken stock with low port curb bits. The western lads and those from the Pacific Coast were more inclined to snap and train their broncs with the hackamore and then later ride with the spade bit. The latter were decidedly loose-rein riders, while the others were a little more inclined to show tight-rein riders in their ranks.

I started and rode for several years the half-breed low port curb. I was riding the small Mustang then and I really gave no thought to my bits. A bit was a bit to me then. Most of the mounts went well and I must say I did ride some humdinging cutting ponies in southwest Texas. Then I drifted down into old Mexico, all through the plateau and down to Tierra Caliente. There I used, as a rule, the Chileno or

Ring Bit. Everybody seemed to use it; the ponies were broke to it; and, being naturally a loose-rein rider, I got along fine. Oh, yes, I ran into some sun-snifters and cold-jaws, but that's to be expected because *all* horses can't be good.

Then, over forty years ago, I drifted into California for the first time, and found the vaqueros there, both paisanos and gringos, riding, as a rule, the Spanish Spade. That mouth port looked plenty severe, sure enough! Yet, by the same token, I also commenced to ride some of the sweetest-mouthed, flash-reined ponies I had ever forked. Well, a man gets used to anything in this world, and it wasn't long before I had discarded my double cinch and was riding a center-fire, and getting me a rawhide reata and using my grass rope for a picket line. Incidentally I was also giving up the idea that I wanted to be a top bronc twister. However, I did get more interested in reining colts, and then it was that I really got all steamed up about the way to use a hackamore properly. It was then only one jump to the spade. And so the argument goes.

The original intention of this book was not so much to discuss the whys and the wherefores, and the pros and cons, and all that palaver about cowboy tools, as it was to name and describe them in detail, and show them in pictures. Yet I always find myself bogging down in some of those discussions I thought I was going to avoid. Well, I guess it's perfectly natural, for there's got to be a difference of opinion in this world or we wouldn't get up enough steam to keep this old apple gravitating. I try to be as fair as I can in all my reflections, and I'm generally able to, because I've been over the length and breadth of Cowland, and a great part of it forty to fifty years ago when cowboys were a little different from what they are today. I've used all rigs and systems, and I've always tried to be a close observer to the different ways they got the same job done in all the various, far-flung corners. I'm not a "native son," so I don't have to get bull-

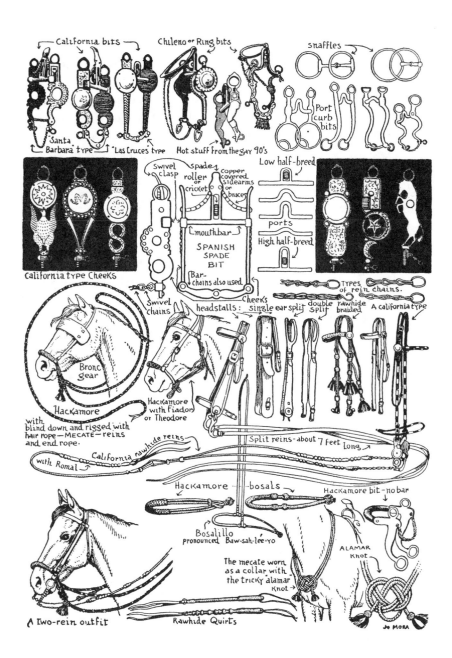

California bits — Chileno or Ring bits — snaffles →

Santa Barbara type — Las Cruces type — Hot stuff from the gay 90's

Port curb bits

California type Cheeks

Swivel clasp — spade roller or cricket — copper covered sidearms or braces

mouthbar

SPANISH SPADE BIT

Bar-chains also used

Low half-breed

ports

High half-breed

Swivel chains

Cheeks

Types of rein chains.

headstalls: single ear — split — double split — rawhide braided

A california type

Bronc gear

Hackamore

with blind down and rigged with hair rope — MECATE — reins and end rope.

Hackamore with Fiador or Theodore

Split reins - about 7 feet long →

California rawhide reins →

with Romal →

Hackamore — bosals →

Hackamore bit - no bar

Bosalillo
pronounced Baw-sah-lee-yo

ALAMAR Knot

The mecate worn as a collar with the tricky alamar knot →

A Two-rein outfit

Rawhide Quirts

JO MORA

headed and loyal to any one locality or to their way of operating.

So, in this matter of bits, I'll say that both sides have their good points and their bad ones, though often the bad ones are really the outcome of ignorance or bungling on the part of the rider, aided and abetted at times by the cussedness of horseflesh.

On a horse that's been properly broken and reined with a hackamore, bitted by a good hand, and ridden by a loose-rein stockman who knows what it's all about, I consider the spade bit tops. It is then anything but cruel, and if you know anything about the anatomy of a horse's mouth you know how it lies and that it does not hurt the sensitive roof. A pony will roll that cricket with all equine phlegm and contentment.

Of course, if you're one of those heavy-handed shorthorns that ride the reins and not the horse (and there are hundreds of such so-called cowboys), you're going to spoil a horse that's bitted with a spade. It's then I will admit that a spade turns into a "stomach pump" and a cruel this and that and whatnot. It sure is . . . but so are many other fine instruments in the hands of the ignorant. For instance, take a hypo needle full of morphine in the hands of a good doctor and it can be an angel of mercy: yet in the fist of some bum in the back room of the old saloon and it can be a different story. Well, it's the same thing with bits. And don't think this just applies to spades, for curbs can be just as cruel in the hands of the ignorant.

If anybody could show me where the majority of curb-bitted stockhorses are well behaved, flash-reined working cow ponies, then I'll take my sombrero off to the curb bit alone and vote to throw the old spade into the discard. But nobody has ever been able to show me any such thing. The truth is, I was never so surprised as I was during some recent trips through the Panhandle and Oklahoma, to see how many stock horses there were packing the craziest assortment of bit combinations. As I stated before, some of these cockeyed contraptions looked more

A hackamore colt

like the inventions of a cowboy Rube Goldberg than of a properly func-
tioning stockman. I rode through those ranges nearly half a century
ago with an outfit that was buying native cow ponies, mustangs, and
Indian ponies. We got some top ones, too; and I rode them all. Yet I
can't remember seeing any of these funny-looking reining devices.
Maybe I couldn't see very well, or maybe I wasn't a close observer.

Anyhow, it set me to thinking and wondering what was the matter.
My conclusions were that the trouble rested with the modern horses
and the way they were broken and trained. Maybe the little, old, cold-
blooded stock horses and mustangs would stand more abuse at the
mouth than our modern hot-bloods will put up with. When the southwestern stockman started to improve his saddle stock, he introduced,
and blended, and experimented with thoroughbreds in Standard stock,
Running, Arabians, Morgans and then even a pinch of Percheron to add
weight and to steady some of the flighty hot-heads. He seemed obsessed
with the modern craze for speed, speed, speed; so, believe me, the Running stock wasn't neglected. In searching for that, I think many of them
forgot that a good cow horse, though he should have a good burst of
speed, was first, last, and always a work horse. He should not be only a
parade horse and a racer. He should have a flash rein, but he should also
have a level head. He shouldn't paw, and rear, and fuss, and take off
when you piled out of the saddle and ran down the rope with the piggin' string in your mouth; or when engaged in any of the countless
pinches a working stockman runs into in his daily work. Now don't tell
me that a brute that has to wear a crazy instrument of torture in his
mouth is a nice, quiet, work horse to depend on. No more, to my notion,
than to choose some pilgrim to teach the local kindergarten that has to
wear a strait-jacket.

Some of those contraptions had gadgets on them to choke off the
wind when the pressure was applied; some had leverages on them long
enough to raise a barn; and there were other schemes, all of them work-

ing on the principle of inflicting great pain to try for results. Well, right on the face of it, those doodads were the insignia of defeat and the proof that those horses were too much for the trainers. There's something wrong somewhere. Maybe the trainers are losing their old-time cunning; or maybe the old way they had of breaking broncs doesn't work with these modern ones. If that is not the case, then some of these hot-bloods are not worth two bits as cow horses. You tell me.

Then again, there's another handicap we must consider, and that is the modern, streamlined efficiency business where things must be done in two months that took the old-timers a year or more. The high price of labor doesn't help much, either. In the old days with the big spreads, in Texas and the Great Plains, when they were getting things ready and

81

organizing for the Spring Round-up, they'd hire a couple of professional twisters for several weeks to start the colts that had come of age to be broken. The cavvy was gathered up into the home corrals, the broncs to be broken were cut out, and the gentle stock was caught up and parcelled out to the cowboys for their individual strings. Then into these strings would go the bombshells as they were "broke" by the twisters. If, alone, a waddie could rope, saddle, and fork a bronc without committing suicide, that critter was broke and went into the working string.

Remember that when a puncher went on round-up, and he'd have to switch to one of these green, rough ones, he couldn't act on him just as a trainer alone; he had no time for that. He had his work to do, some of it difficult and specialized. He might have to do some fast heading off and turning of wild cows in very rough country; he might have to run down that rope after the catch, and a thousand and one tricky stunts that were none too easy on gentle mounts. Imagine the rein those snakes had. Imagine the jack-pots those cowboys got into trying to accomplish these stunts on stiff-necked, half-baked broncs. It was playing with dynamite, sure enough. And yet, as a rule, those broncs would wiggle through a season somehow or other, and, in a way, just about teach themselves. Now and then you'd pick up a good pony with a fair rein, out of these. And most of those little rascals really had "cow sense." It's a fact, and they' take to the work like they really enjoyed it. They got pretty canny and knew a lot of what was wanted. Pick out a cow to cut from the bunch, and some of those ponies would do the job practically by themselves, and the riders generally gave them their heads. They did the job in their own way, and they got right stubborn about it if the rider tried to interfere with their routine. It was mighty cute to see the interest and intelligence of those ponies. But it is *not* my idea of a good cow pony. I want the pony to do things my way and under my guidance. When my mount knows more than I do about how things should be done, then it's high time I quit and let him do the worrying. But, to sum it up briefly, I don't think the modern hot-bloods can be successfully broken with that system.

Personally, I would never start a colt I thought much of with anything but a hackamore. I think it's dead wrong to start them with a bit in the mouth. There's generally some pretty rough going those first days, and I want to keep that mouth sensitive and unhurt. Then when the bronc has been gentled and thoroughly reined to the hackamore, all I have to do is to slip the bit into that mouth and teach him how to pack it. He already knows how to neck rein. Whereas if you start in with a bit in the bronc's mouth, you are bound to jerk him roughly when he bucks; or when you're obliged to yank his head around; or to set him up. You just can't help abusing him at times, and this naturally tends to raw or lacerate that mouth, especially if the breaker is heavy handed. Then it's liable to get calloused and the bronc gets used to the pain, and right there you may be making another cold-jaw brute or a nervous, tender-mouthed wreck out of possibly a fine prospect.

But that's the way it goes. Sometimes I really think that part of the trouble is with the stubborn pride of some trainers: they hate to admit there's anything wrong with their systems and that the other method is better. They seem to stick to the loyal theory that if it was good enough for grandpaw it should be good enough for them. But grandpaw's cavvy was not made up of the hot-blooded blends they are trying to turn into cow ponies.

The types and designs of bits and bit shanks are gradually getting more alike throughout the length and breadth of cattleland. Modern ways are breaking down the old barriers of distance with their varying local characteristics. There are no distances these days, while the movies and the rodeo shows are doing much to standardize. The spade bit is getting less popular, and even those characteristic old California bit shanks are slowly blending into another type. The advent of rustless steel is also doing a lot to change appearances. When I was a kid, when we bought a California bit, with its conchas, buttons and inlays of silver, the steel was blued; yet many of us preferred the brown background that came from its being rusted. We'd put the new bit in the horse trough to start the rusting, get rid of the blueing, and lay the foundation for the brown color. And to my notion, nothing is handsomer than good silver work with the background of brown steel. Silver on rustless steel lacks class, and looks tinny.

Not so long ago, in the catalogues of the saddle stores on the Coast, you'd see page after page of those fine-looking California style bits; some swivel-jawed, some rigid. All had chains attached for the reins to fasten to. Reins were closed and of braided rawhide with buttons, 4, 8, 12 and even 16 plait. The buttons, too, were a matter of taste: some with very few, others with many. There was also a long piece, made just like the reins, with two snappers at one end for quirting. This is called the Romal and it loops or buttons to the hand end of the reins, and may be readily attached or detached when roping. Then these catalogues might have a page or half-page showing a few curb bits, Eastern style.

Of course, quite the opposite were the catalogues of the saddle houses east of the Rockies. The many bits shown there were low port curbs of different patterns, and no chains. The single, flat-leather split reins buckled right on to the bit shank. They, too, gave a little space in turn to the "other" kinds of bits, and generally showed a cheap factory-turned-out spade and a Mexican ring bit. These, I imagine, were shown in case some dude or sucker wanted one to send home as a souvenir of the Wild West.

On the Coast, the vaqueros preferred a narrow-cheeked headstall, generally round, even though their bit shanks were wide and heavy, with large conchas, much silver inlay, and even heavy bars connecting the shanks. On the other hand, the curb-bit waddies liked wider,

84

heavier headstalls, and some of them were very wide and heavy, even though their bit shanks were small and often very narrow.

The Coast vaquero never threw the reins and romal over the horse's head to leave him standing. He tied with his mecate. The split-rein cowboy dismounted, let the reins fall to the ground, and the ponies were broke to stand without tying. Generally it worked, though sometimes, under unusual conditions, it naturally didn't. A pony was supposed to step on the reins if he tried to make off, and he generally did. However, some got very wise to this procedure, and they'd raise their muzzles high and far to one side, and they could scamper away plenty fast.

The ring bit, often called a Chileno, is just a severe curb. In place of the curb strap the lower jaw goes into a steel ring that is hung from the top of the mouth port. With one who rides the reins or is very heavy-handed, this bit can be quite severe: but on a well-reined horse with a loose-rein rider, there is positively nothing wrong with it.

The cowboy's hat, from earliest days to this, has gone up and down the gamut of period or local styles. However, it has always been a felt hat with a good brim. Sometimes this brim has been of medium width and then again very wide. Sometimes with a curl, sometimes flat. Generally it was stiff enough to stand the pressure of a high wind, or that created when "jamming the breeze" at full speed. In the old days there was a sombrero, very popular on some ranges, that had an exceedingly wide brim. This, as it grew old, often got quite wobbly; and I might say that the abuses a frontier hat received would tend to wobble anything made of felt. The waddies would push the front brim up and back against the crown and it would often hold pretty well in place, especially if facing the breeze. However, it was also mighty temperamental, and if the breeze caught it from some other angle, it would snap down and over the owner's eyes like a trap. Many of the old frontiersmen, cowboys, trappers, and plainsmen threaded a piece of whang or rawhide through little slots cut close to the outer rim in an attempt to stiffen it. I have even seen, on a couple of occasions, the brim of this type stiffened with baling-wire.

The crowns of the cowboy's hat have also followed the ups and downs of fashion: low, medium, and high. Time was when the high-crowned "ten-gallon" hat was popular mostly in the Southwest. However, for the past quarter century it has been "the Hat" in nearly all corners of Cowboy Land. It kept getting bigger and bigger as the movie cowboys, who set many of the fashions these days, kept boosting the ante till we worried lest it might turn into a tent, instead of a hat for a workingman on a horse. However, at the date of this writing, I think that the turn has come, as it does with all abuses, and the trend is more now for the handier sizes.

In the matter of creasing the crown, it has also been according to taste, though there have been styles prevalent at different periods and at different localities. Crowns were often worn without any dent or crease; or with the old conventional four dents that brought the top to a sharp peak; or just two dents, the top rolling over; or the long crease from the top down the front; or just the reverse, two narrow creases forming a roll down the front. I have even received letters from movie cowboys asking for suggestions in this matter. If things keep on at this rate, someone should start a style department for tired cowboys in some fancy society magazine. Ho, hum! Our poor waddies certainly have their troubles these days, and we should give them a hand whenever possible. You know, their calling is sure rough on manicures.

This same modern trend toward standardization applies strongly these days to the cowboy chaps (pronounced "shaps"). When I first drifted into California I had a pair of Texas wing chaps and I was quite a curiosity. The boys all wore the angora closed leg, though sometimes they were of dog or bear pelt: black, white, and orange were the popular colors. Later on, at our early rodeo shows, I saw some enthusi-

When angoras went the limit.

asts with their angoras dyed green and pink. Then in the 20's and 30's when the wing chap came into more and more general vogue, the angoras had their swan song and, boy! how they sang. They started spotting them and then made them with a big wing. Now when you cover a surface of that area with prime, long, curly angora, I'm telling you you've got something. When those buckaroos waddled along as dismounted bipeds with those mammoth contraptions on, they sure looked funny. And funny is the word for it.

The closed (shotgun leg) fringed chap was the popular chap in the old days on the prairies, the 70's, 80's and 90's, but it lost its great appeal with the turn of the century. The belts to the old-style chaps were straight across, instead of the various form-fitting curves of the modern, and were worn much looser, with the top of the leg not fitting snugly at the crotch. For that reason, when in the saddle, the belts were inclined to work up around the waist. Modern ones fit much better. Then, too, the old ones were generally well laced together in front, where ours today are just fastened with a thin bit of whang. This, in case the chap belt gets caught over the horn when the going is rough, will easily break and possibly save the rider from a nasty accident.

However, for popularity, the winged leather chap has swept the field. They are made up now from the plainest type without even conchas or outside pockets, to the fanciest creations of applied, many-colored leather work of initials, names, brands, animals and human figures, etc. etc. Even silver ornaments beside the conchas. Of course all this fancy stuff was influenced by the movies, the rodeo shows, and the fiesta parades. You'd scarcely call some of them the chaps of a working cowboy. I know many of the owners of these fancy folderols never saw a range cow in its native habitat. But it all keeps up the interest in "Western rigs" and horses, and it gives much employment to many fine craftsmen. So let 'em boom!

Formerly, winged chaps were worn buckled all the way down, with the exception of the one at the knee which was never fastened so that there might be greater freedom in bending the leg. Nowadays, they are

JO MORA   Wearing chinks.

seldom made with buckles beyond the knee, and the lower half hangs loose. The "Cheyenne leg," which is the lower inside leg piece cut away at a curve, is very popular, and deserves to be. When a peeler, these days, scratches a pitching bronco, his chaps, unfastened below the knees, flap around plenty and plainly show the lower legs of the rider. They certainly help to fan that bronc.

Chinks, or Armitas, are a kind of skeleton chap, and were worn quite a bit on some coast ranges and in Nevada. They are generally made of buckskin, the sides and bottoms often fringed. They are made up like a carpenter's long apron without a bib. The fronts were fastened with thongs or light straps around the leg, tied or snapped. Personally, I like them immensely for light brush and very hot weather.

III

he evolution of the stock saddle is hardly an evolution. It is really more of a refining of details than anything else. Some time ago, I was looking over an old saddle that dated back at least to the 50's, and the darned thing looked positively modern in lines. It had a flat horn top, five inches in diameter, and a fairly narrow stem. By the way, the Mexican type horn is coming into quite a bit of popularity these last few years. The one on this old saddle was the image of some of the modern ones. Personally I like the Mexican type horn with the heavy, thick stem, made with the proper pinch to the front angle so that it will not jam the rope, yet has just enough bite to hold a right smart jerk even with one dally. Of course many ropers wouldn't have one of these on a bet, but the majority of these objectors have never tried one that was properly made. I used to feel the same way myself. The all-metal horn is only good for the hard and fast roper. On a narrow necked horn I like to wind a soft cotton rope, as it gives a fine bite for dally work.

On the old saddle I mentioned, there was a slanting cantle much like those on the old McClelland army saddles, and it had a hand slot in the center. I've seen others of these old types with two hand slots, a style that was used much on Mexican saddles of that period. The tree was covered with rawhide only, and was Spanish rig. It had the original old stirrup leathers, only 1½ inches wide, with no rosaderos, or fenders, and the stirrups were missing. There was no other covering on it, no skirts, no jockeys. Naturally, it looked very much like the old Mexican tree, yet the character of the cinch rigging, though Spanish rigged, did not look Mexican. It had a light ring on which to knot the narrow latigos, and not with a tongue for buckling the very wide latigos of the Mexican rig. Of course, we must always remember that our stock saddles originated from the Mexican, and while the Texan was refining his to suit his requirements or notions, the plainsmen, the trappers, in fact most of the early frontiersmen of the West, got their horned saddles from the Mexican in the Santa Fe trade and thereabout and later from California. Those early exposed rig saddles were meant to be ridden with a heavy leather housing (mochila) covering the seat. These were removable and had openings in them to slip the horn and cantle through. Later on, our own saddlers made a saddle somewhat on those lines. That is, it had a plain housing over all, but it was stitched on and was not removable. The boys called these Old Mother Hubbards. They were a pretty good saddle, too, but they did not survive the changing fashions. At this writing, I know of one such which is in daily use with the dudes on the H F Bar Ranch in Wyoming. It is still a good, serviceable old saddle and a comfortable rig to ride. An interesting detail to it is that the stirrups are made entirely of leather, no wood entering into the construction. I show a sketch of it.

To write of the many slight, gradual changes from the original Mexican to our modern stock saddle, would get very technical and a bit dry and confusing reading to the average reader not familiar with the Western rigs. However, I think the new or old student of Cowboy Lore will welcome a set of progressive sketches showing this "evolution" in a visual manner. This I show for your possible interest, and also a sketch of the original source, the Mexican saddle, with its complete nomenclature in Spanish, that you may study and compare them if you wish.

The most radical departure in our gradual refining was the advent of the swelled fork. These new creations busted in on us at the turn of the century with their great, heavy, swelled shoulders that measured 15 or 16 inches through. I'll never forget the first time I saw one. I was camped on the Puerco with a Babbitt outfit, and two of us rode in to Holbrook, Arizona, on company business. This took but a short time, and then we naturally gravitated over to the old Apache House bar to

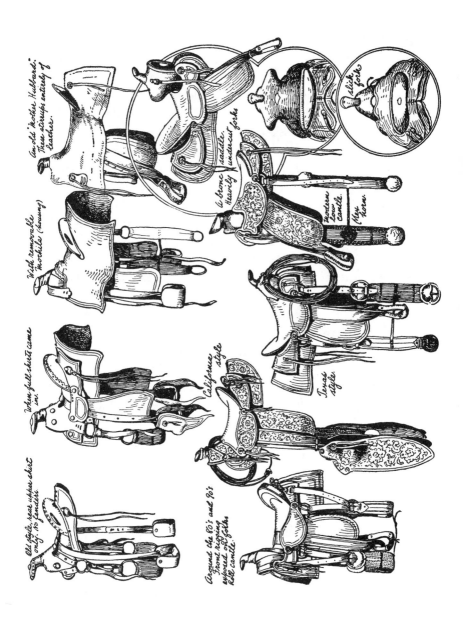

An old "Mother Hubbard." These stirrups entirely of leather.

A bronc saddle. Heavily undercut forks.

Texas low cantle. Nye horn.

with forks

With removable "hoodies" (bucking)

When full skirt came in.

California style

Texas style

Old style, wide upper skirt only, no fender.

Around the 80's and 90's. Front rigging warned out forks. Roll cantle.

get a bit fortified for the hazardous return trip to camp. The place was quite empty, except for a lone tobacco drummer who was telling the latest stories to the bar tender. He seemed lonesome, and thirsty, and most sociably inclined. So we hoisted plenty of snorts together, and in the course of our noisy, good-natured conversation, he declared he'd bet a quart of the best whiskey in the house that he had a better saddle than either one of us. Well, we were riding good, plain working saddles, though nothing fancy enough to back up on a bet; yet we knew there was a catch somewhere, and the generous amount of merry mucilage that we had tucked under our belts made us ready to back Uncle Jed's plough mare for the Kentucky Derby. So we took him on, and told him to produce his entry. He said we'd have to walk down to the railroad station, as he had it checked there. You see, he had already finished his business in town and was just laying over waiting for the Overland, which was late, to take him to Flagstaff.

So, down to the depot we all waddled, after the drummer had mort-gaged the enterprise for the quart bottle to take with us in case a rattle-snake or a sudden chill or something equally dangerous disputed the trail with us. Anyhow, he finally got the saddle out of check, and it was well put up in a gunny sack. Then he cut the stitches and hauled it out for our inspection. There it was, with the great clumsy shoulders of the early types, measuring about 16 through the forks. We gave it the laugh, for it looked funny enough to us, and kidded him that some dude humorist had had it built as a joke, and that he'd been the sucker to fall for it and pay real money. And, to be frank about it, that's just what we thought. However, when we examined it further, our experienced eyes told us plainly that here was a sturdy, strong, exceptionally well-made stock saddle. I can't remember the name of the maker, but it was some Denver outfit. It had been used, too; and used hard.

But we couldn't kid that drummer for a second, because he didn't seem to care much about money, declaring this all went on his expense account as he'd bought it to take back East to his boss who collected odd saddles. He further stated he had just bought it a couple of days past, at Gallup, New Mexico, from a stranded and busted cowboy from Colorado, who had gambled away his stake at the Monte table of one of the local emporiums, and was pitifully drunk and practically in the gutter.

We were just about to take a snifter from our fresh bottle in commiseration for that poor cowboy, steeped in sin, who had to sell his saddle (which is the last resort of a desperate puncher) when two waddies we knew well rode up and joined us. They had been riding for several seasons at the Tonto, and were just drifting north, seeking new ranges and new excitement. They joined us in the bottle and in kidding, or trying to kid, that drummer. However, one of them took me aside and whispered that the foreman of the outfit they had just quit had recently returned from delivering a trainload of steers at Kansas City, and that he had told them about these new saddles, and swore we would all be riding them soon. How well he prophesied.

That was many years ago, well over forty, and I've seen the swelled forks run up and down the full gamut of cockeyed fancy, and some lulus certainly have been turned out. I've seen them as wide as 22 inches. Of course, everything that's abnormal sooner or later finds its level, and, though by no means have the swelled forks been discarded, and I don't think ever will, yet the trend now is more towards the slick forks. Hundreds of these have lately been made and sold where, a few years back, they were as dead as dodos. There is positively no argument against the fact that the modern bronc saddle with the *undercut* and *back-bulged* forks, the steep heavily dished cantle, the short tree, and the shorter stirrup leathers is of the greatest assistance to the twister. I guess that saddle will stay with us as long as Western horses back up their convictions with bucking; though for all-around chores on the ranch and range, and for fast or heavy roping, it is *not* a good rig, for there is where the rider needs freedom of action.

The extreme bronc saddle is not allowed in the organized rodeo shows. At these, a medium type, called the association tree, has been adopted. These saddles are furnished the boys who compete, as they are not allowed to ride their own rigs. So, the lads who have their eyes peeled for the contest purses do their practising on this type tree. Personally, I feel free to be severely critical of an exhibition rider's technique, the closeness of his seat, the freedom of his scratching, and the looseness of his style in general. That is exhibition stuff, and he's up there riding for show; people have paid money to see him; and he gets good money in prizes if he's got what it takes. However, for the common or garden variety of hero who has to ride broncs for his daily bait, he can cinch an elephant's howdah, with hot and cold running water, on to his bronc for all of me, and more power to 'im. He's entitled to all the breaks, every one of them.

It would be so romantic for me to boast, yes, even hint, that I've been one of those big, HE, "gimme a bronc for breakfast" boys. But murder will out, sooner or later, and I'd hate to have to hem and haw at the last roundup to cover my bluff. The truth is that some of my sourest recollections are the result of that bronc for breakfast stuff. Those bitter cold mornings before sun-up, trying to bolt a bait through chattering teeth, and (if you had to ride one of your rough string) casting a look over into the semidarkness where that equine criminal they called a broke pony was standing there quiet enough, his head down, his eyes staring cold, every hair on his body sticking up like a door mat, and a hump in his back that tilted the rear skirts of the saddle so's you could hide a hat under them. Forking a hostile hurricane deck when cold and stiff is not what I'd call ideal conditions for making a good ride. Well, I'll confess that after my first couple of years, all my bronc riding was done because it was positively necessary and certainly not from choice.

I was one of those that clung to the slick forks the longest and was

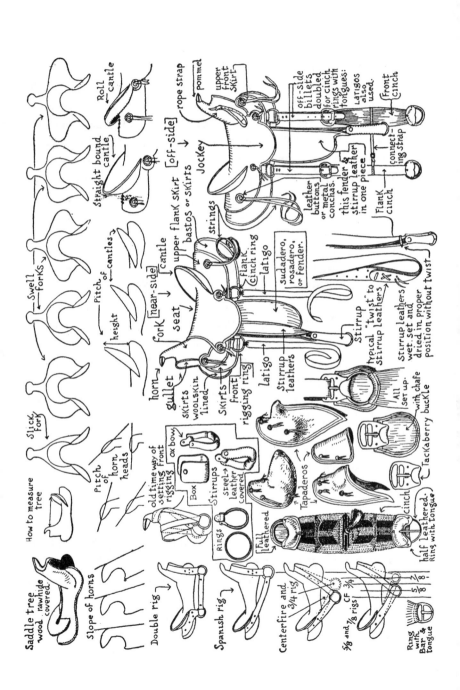

Saddle tree wood, rawhide covered.

How to measure tree

Slope of horns

Pitch of horn heads

Slick fork

Swell forks

Pitch of cantles

height

Roll cantle

Straight bound cantle

Double rig

Spanish rig

Centerfire and ¾ rig

⅝ and ⅞ rigs

CF ¾

⅝ ⅝ ⅝

Ring with Bar & Tongue

old-time way of setting front rigging

ox bow

Box

Stirrups

Rings

Full leathered

Stirrups steel leather covered

Tapaderos

half leathered. Ring with tongue

cinch

All set up with chafe

Jackaberry buckle

horn

gullet

Skirts woolskin lined

Skirts front rigging ring

latigo

Stirrup leathers

Stirrup

typical "twist" to stirrup leathers

Stirrup leathers wet set and dried in proper position without twist

fork [near-side]

seat

Cantle

upper flank skirt

bastos or skirts

strings

Flank cinching ring

latigo

sudadero, rosadero, or fender.

rope strap

pommel

upper front skirt

off-side billets doubled for cinch rings with tongues: latigos also used.

front cinch

Jockey

leather buttons or metal conchas.

this fender & stirrup leather in one piece

connecting strap

Flank cinch

really past my prime for topping broncs when I got my first swelled fork. I always started my own colts and tried to ride as clean as possible for my own satisfaction: yet when the bad ones really bothered me I never hesitated for a second to take every advantage I could. Generally I tied a folded and rolled slicker or mackinaw back of the slick forks for a bucking roll. And if my bronc proved too much of a rowdy, I never hesitated to hobble my stirrups or stretch leather. Any fool that's got the guts to crawl the bad ones has my complete respect. I never knew what it was to really lose my grit with broncos till I had one final argument that softened me up for good.

I had broken and reined a colt for an outfit and had worked him thoroughly through the Spring rodeo season, and he was as neat a prospect as I had seen for many a day. We named him Champagne . . . plenty good with lots of bubbles. I left that Summer and was gone for over a year. When I returned to that locality, I had been married, and soon settled down on a little ranch of my own. I wanted a nice, well-mannered pony for my wife, and naturally I thought of that Champagne colt. I got in touch with the ranch owner and found out that the pony had been spoiled by a rattle-brained vaquero and an unfortunate accident. That part is too long a story, but, anyhow, the pony was spoiled.

I guess I thought I was pretty smart in my way of handling horses, and I had known this pony from his bronc days. So I bought him fairly cheap. Then I tried all my tricks on him for over a year and never even made a hopeful improvement on him. I finally had to ride him with a double rein, and when I started the day with him, I'd give him a good whirl at the end of the mecate, then I'd rein him up fairly short with the mecate reins and give these a couple of half hitches on the horn so he couldn't get his head down. He'd allow you to get perfectly seated, in fact he would not budge till you leaned forward or indicated with your spurs that you wanted him to move. Then he'd crow-hop ahead a few jumps, a couple of waltz steps to the side like a crab, and then he'd straighten out for the rest of the day, as fine and gentle a saddle pony as I owned. But if you didn't limber him up and keep his head tied, you had as pretty an argument on your hands as you'd want: fast, tricky and twisting.

Well, it was the same old story. I got careless one day, and being late for a date in town, I hurried over to the hitching rail where Champagne had been standing saddled for over a couple of hours. My mind was on my date, not my horse, as I untied him from the rail, and swung aboard without the usual and necessary ceremonies. Well, he didn't wait for a declaration of hostilities: he just exploded and how! I was hanging to the horn, my left foot solid in the stirrup, my right knee smack up against the back of the cantle while my right spurred heel was hooked tight over his rump where I had clamped down hard when the eruption started. I positively couldn't let go that hold or pull over into the saddle. Of course this all happened in seconds, and he bucked hard and fast straight ahead for about fifty yards to a dry creek, plunged through the willows, and off the steep bank. This operation shook me loose and I landed ploughing along on the back of my neck and shoulders in that creek gravel. I was then really past the hard bronc-riding age, and when I woke up and finally convinced myself that I was still alive, I decided that messing around with spoiled horses didn't pay dividends. By all the rules of acrobatics I should have been killed, for I left a furrow in that creek bottom six feet long, and a couple of hours later, in town at the end of a fast fifteen mile ride, my wife picked gravel from the collar and shoulders of my flannel shirt. How I didn't snap my neck off the way I landed is hard to explain. I guess the Lord looks after the feebleminded, or the Devil takes care of his own. Anyhow, somebody was pulling for me that day.

I decided to get rid of that horse as a saddler and break him to drive, though he was a trifle small for a good, upstanding buggy horse.

So, having arrived at that conclusion, and being perfectly human, I
made up my mind I'd give him just one more ride, give him his head,
and let him buck till he was willing to stop on his own accord. So the
next morning I didn't tie his head up, but I was ready for him as I knew
every move he would make. I had positively no fear of the outcome, as
I gathered the reins and took my hold on the mane. Then I turned the
stirrup to receive my foot, and . . . well, it's hard to explain what happened. Something suddenly sparked through me that I can't describe;
but I knew I was licked, thoroughly licked. I should have quit right
then and there and followed that impulse, or hunch, or whatever you
might call it. But I didn't stop a second in my routine motions, and my
foot went into the stirrup, I eased into the saddle, caught my off stirrup
properly, and then Champagne's head disappeared as he made a couple
of fast bucks ahead with a quick twist to the left. Any rider should have
sat that out, for he really had not as yet got warmed up to his performance, yet I just poured out of that saddle and landed in a trash pile of
ashes and barrel staves. Any farmer should have stuck those first few
jumps, yet I knew just what was coming and what the answer was going
to be. My bronc riding days were over. That was plenty of years ago,
and, with knowledge and intention, I've never forked a bad one since.

In the matter of stirrups, the Texans discarded the Mexican type
and introduced an assorted and varying collection. There was the bent
wooden stirrup that often ran to very wide widths, 4, 5, and even 6
inches. On many of these the sides were the same width as the bottoms
and we used to call them "dog houses." Sometimes they narrowed
toward the top where the bolt came. Then with the years came a varied
lot of wooden Ox Bow stirrups. All good stirrups are leather-bound at
the bottoms and also around the bolt and roller. The stirrups themselves
are often entirely covered with leather or rawhide. Sometimes they are
covered on the outside, all around the sides and bottom, with a strip
of thin galvanized iron, or zinc, or brass. Then, too, the boys often rode

100

just an iron ring. An innovation of later years are those made of aluminum alloy. It would take a volume in itself to try to enumerate the varying types of stirrups that the cowboy has used and is using today. However, bear in mind that the steel stirrup of the "English" type has never been worn by our stockmen.

Many riders wear a hood or leather covering to their stirrups which is called the "tapadero," "or "taps" for short. This means in Spanish, "something that covers." There have been many different types of taps throughout the years, and in each type also varying cuts and styles. A real old-timer was a piece of leather fitting snugly at the top and slanting down and forward at an angle to give plenty of foot room at the toe. As it curved back it was fastened to the sides of the stirrup with strings and leather saddle buttons in pairs (the upper one smaller than the lower) and sometimes with metal conchas. The lower rear portion of the leather sides was finished off longer than the front, and came more or less to a point. This type, the simplest of all taps, had many variations.

Then there is the full-covered short tap, the best of which are nowadays made in one piece. They come down the front close to the stirrup a short way, then poke straight out at almost a right angle, the two sides rolling down and meeting at the bottom where they are stitched together, snugging up right back to the heel. The bottoms can be made very shallow, medium, or full. In some sections we call these "bulldogs." Another type is very similar to this one in the upper part, but instead of the short sides curving under and meeting, the sides are very long and fall straight down, sometimes as high as 26 inches. If this type is made by a good saddler from good patterns, they can be the smartest, handsomest things you'd ever want to see. Both of these two last-mentioned types are generally lined with sheep pelt, and, being so thoroughly closed, keep the feet warm and dry in heavy winter weather.

Another type of stirrup and tapadero that I must mention, though

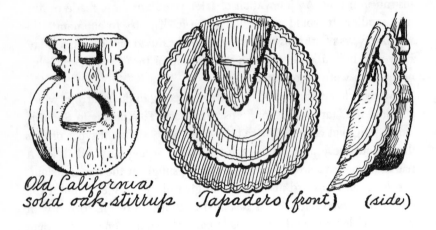

*Old California
solid oak stirrup*   *Tapadero (front)*   *(side)*

they do not belong to the United States Cowboy period, were those worn by the California vaquero "before the Gringo." Though they may have been used by some very early cowmen, the early frontiersmen and plainsmen used them considerably, as they got them with their horned saddles from the Californians and the Spaniards in the Santa Fe trade. They were all of one general type though of varied detail. The stirrups were carved out of a solid piece of hard wood. The holes for the foot were small, as the Spanish colonial stockman has generally been a "toe rider," and did not thrust his foot deep into the stirrup to the heel the way we do. Some of these stirrups were inlaid with silver in very interesting designs. The tapaderos were large and round, and as but little room was needed beyond the small foot hole, they came down pretty straight and curved back but slightly. They were made up of three pieces of leather, two circular (one larger than the other) and one triangular. The accompanying sketch shows this type very clearly, both the stirrup and the tapadero.

The rigging of the stock saddle is of two types, single cinch and double cinch; and then each type has its variations. The original Mexican saddle was "Spanish rigged," which means that the cinch was hung directly down from the forks. Well, your Texan didn't fancy this style with his chosen method of hard and fast roping, so he added another cinch farther back, and that was then called the "double rig." He intended to have that saddle stay in place no matter what happened.

On the other hand, the early Californians did not fancy the cinch hanging directly down from the forks, as it gave too much play to the saddle for them, and also tended to gall up at the elbow easier, when it slid forward on a low-withered horse. So they moved the cinch ring back and hung it at the middle of the tree, but still held to one cinch only. This was called California or center-fire style. Then, a little later, they commenced certain variations in the exact hang of this single cinch, moving it forward a trifle. So now we have the center fire, the ⅝, the ¾ and the ⅞ rig.

All these rigs are good, depending on individual tastes, types of work to be done, and different conformations of horses. For the hard and fast roper the double rig is the only thing; and the single cinch for the dally man. Of course, with a horse that's inclined to be a bit pot-bellied and low-withered, you can't hold a saddle in just the proper place, I don't care what rig you ride . . . double or single. Naturally, with a double rig, you can set the flank cinch to lie on the back curve of a pot-belly and then cinch it up tight. But who wants to ride a horse in a day's work over rough ground with that kind of a corset on?

For the single cinch rigs, I think one of the real improvements has been the developing of the various new styles of flat-plate rigging. The old-time center-fires were often made up with what I considered a mighty primitive rig. I refer to that clumsy bunch that came under the rider's leg from the aggregate of rigging, ring and under-stirrup leather through it, latigo wrappings and bulky knot with its loose end looped back. It all was not what one might call streamline efficiency. Truth is,

103

it very often caused ring sores on the ponies and didn't feel any too soothing to a tired rider's leg. With these flat plates, the stirrup leather generally passes over it and not through, which gives them unhampered freedom. They are really efficient arrangements and a decided improvement. I ride now a single ¾ rig, with a double billet on the off side, and this calls for a buckle tongue to my cinch ring; while on the near side I use a specially cast, heavy bronze Tackaberry buckle. This rig I show in my sketch. I have ridden this type for over thirty years, and I've found it tops in every way, and certainly quick and handy for saddling or unsaddling.

Cowboy saddle cinches are made up of different materials: cotton, fishcord, mohair, horsehair (preferably mane), canvas or leather. The two last mentioned are generally used as flank cinches on double rigs. The rings may be plain or with buckle tongues. These rings are generally (though not always) leathered to keep them from direct contact with the horse's barrel. Sometimes the hair cinches are woven, but as a rule they are made up with the material in separate cord strands and held in place at the center by a cross bar of the same material. Or they may have three bars, in which case the center is generally in design with a diamond shape and often with a large hair tassel hanging from its center. Horsehair and mohair cinches are generally made up in various colors, and a well-made one is a mighty pretty article. The average width for single rigs is 5 or 6 inches. For double rigs they are narrower, as a wide front cinch would be very apt to chafe and gall a pony back of the elbows. In this rig the flank cinch is often very narrow; sometimes a mere 2-inch strap. This rig also has a narrow little strap, buckling in the center, the ends attached to the middles of the cinches. This allows the space between the cinches to be regulated, and also keeps the flank cinch from crawling back on a horse that's inclined to be "snipe-gutted."

When I was riding in Arizona, I bought a pair of woven cinches from the Navajos, made out of Germantown wool, and they were the prettiest things you ever saw. They were good and serviceable, too, but I only used them when I wanted to put on a little dog. In those days the Navajos used that type of cinch almost exclusively. Personally, I like a cinch made of more open texture: they don't cake up so readily with sweat and dirt.

I remember, in more recent years, I loaned one of my saddles to a ranch that was mounting a string of dudes to ride in the parade of a big rodeo show. This was one of our extra saddles, but it had a very fine mohair cinch. Anyhow, it was a long time getting back to my hands. One day I had occasion to need it, loaning it to a friend who was to ride in our party. He dusted it off and saddled a good, quiet old horse of ours; but when he started off, this old veteran pony humped his back, switched his tail, and acted like hostilities might commence at any moment. On investigating, I finally found that my mohair cinch had been lifted, and a new, cowtail one substituted. It was positively the coarsest, stiffest thing I had ever seen. In fact I didn't know that cowtail could be that wiry. That old pony didn't take much of a fancy to that prickly business on his belly, and none of us blamed him for it. I guess it had been given to me in thanks for the loan of that saddle. And such things do often happen.

The very old saddles generally had strings at the forks to tie the lariat on the off side, and the tie rope on the near. But it isn't every rider that knows how to tie a real good knot that will hold a heavy coil of rope with the constant jiggle of a pony in action, and still be available for instant use without fussing or picking knots. Many a good lass rope was dropped and lost. So the next improvement was a wider single strap with a slot cut at the end. One could snug the lariat close to the fork, take several turns with this strap and then, when the length was right, slip the slot over the horn, and there was your string, perfectly fast, yet ready for instant use. The next improvement over this was a strap and buckle. Modern saddles are made either way, though oftener with the buckle. Then, another mighty handy gadget is a snap placed at the rear jockey button, for hanging the quirt or spurs when not in use.

The old Mexican saddles had big square skirts with large saddle bags built right in, but when the Texan commenced making up his own outfits he soon discarded these. The American cowboy that followed him was never much of a hand for saddle bags, either. I don't mean to state that saddle bags were never used, for they were to a certain limited extent, but they were an extra with him and easily removed. The flaps of these were either plain leather, or embossed, or with a covering of bear, angora, or any pelt that might take his fancy. Sometimes these flaps were quite long and made a very doggie showing. But the boys, as a rule, when they had something extra to take along that was too much for the pants or vest pockets, would roll it in a gunny sack or into the folds of their slicker, snug up close to the back of the cantle, and tie it down with the saddle strings.

I wouldn't need more than the fingers on one hand to tally the water canteens I've seen cowboys packing in fifty years. I don't think I'd need all those fingers. I guess it was because we knew the ranges we rode, and even if they were dry and the water holes few and far between, we figured that if the pony that packed us could stand it, we sure could. Besides, who wanted a water bottle banging a tattoo, anyhow? That might do for mounted soldiers but not for cowboys.

Our stock saddles are made up all plain leather, or stamped, or embossed. Sometimes the absolutely unadorned ones are made up with the rough side of the leather out. These make fine bronc saddles. The simplest ornamentation is the border stamp; then comes the checker or basket stamp; and then the flower embossed. Of late, with the rodeo shows and their parades, the popular fiestas that are getting to be annual community events, and the marked enthusiasm and boom for the Western rig and the Western way of riding, our saddle designers and craftsmen have positively run riot on the use of silver and even gold for the adornment of the saddles. You need a pair of strong specks to see the leather on some of these new creations. Horns, forks, and cantles are often completely encased in solid silver, highly embellished with motifs of horses, cattle, lions, cowboy figures, birds, flowers, stars, what-nots, and even whole family portrait groups of many figures. Such saddles are grand affairs, I guess, though they do lose their identity as stock saddles. Then again, it's all a matter of taste. Personally, I do like a good dash of silver on my spurs and bits, and headstalls, and saddles. But I like this on my everyday working rig. I never owned a show outfit for fiesta days, and I always like to feel I can take after a runaway in the thick brush without fear of amputating Grandma's silver nose from the bas relief.

My notion of what's tops is an old-time California bit shank on rustable steel, with a good silver concha and inlays; good-sized silver conchas on lightweight round leather headstall; all-silver string conchas on the saddle and taps, and initials or brand in silver at the back of cantle. That's all for silver. However, I do admire fine flower embossing on the leather, preferably that small-scale wild-rose pattern. When saddle leather is just encrusted with this type of design well done, and has taken on the color and shine of constant use, and is set off with dashes of silver as already indicated, I don't think there is anything handsomer in the cowboy wardrobe. I don't particularly care for the use of full, realistic cowboy scenes done in the leather. To me they are just so many illustrations and not designs, though I've seen some that were mighty well done. But that, too, is all a matter of personal taste. There's no rule as to what should or should not be used. The old-style saddles had a certain standard character, even including the gorgeously embossed ones, that just seemed to radiate the old Western range. I guess that's why, sentimentally, I hate to see some of these modern changes, like scrapping the old horse and buggy Constitution and the Bill of

Rights. But the world rolls on and styles change, so why criticize the other hombre? If a guy wants to come down to breakfast in his plug hat, white tie and tails, why, that's his own business; and the neighbors shouldn't pass it around that he's just sifted in and hasn't been to bed yet. Even if it's a good bet the first guess was right.

The under parts of the main saddle skirts are lined with sheep wool-skin, and the saddle itself is placed on the horse's back over a blanket or pad. The sheepskin, besides making things a bit softer, also keeps the saddle from crawling. Very often, when a twister is saddling a bronc for his first topping off, and the critter is furnishing too many wiggles for the adjusting of a blanket, the saddle is cinched on without anything under it. A bronc's first ride is seldom of great duration, and a well-lined saddle should not hurt the back, but a good protection, for longer durations, should be under the saddle otherwise.

Old-timers generally used an ordinary blanket, folded to size required. A single blanket, if of wool; a double one, if of cotton. Sometimes a cut burlap sack was used next to the skin and under the other. A very few cowboys used the graduated felt saddle pad. Then there are the heavy curled hair pads, built like a "corona" for round skirts, and many of them with leather chafes for latigo wear. Later, the popularity of the Navajo saddle blanket (single or double) took hold in all corners of the ranges. If these are well made with the proper weave, they are hard to beat for the purpose, being stiff enough to avoid wrinkling, and open enough to avoid overcaking from sweat. They wash well, too.

The double-cinch boys folded their blankets very large and let them hang far down the sides of the pony's barrel; the single-cinch boys, in old California style, folded theirs so that mighty little, if at all, showed beyond the edges of the saddle skirts. A very popular article for this style was the carpet "corona" worn over the blanket. They were open on top most of the way, leather-bound, and many with sheep-wool lining. If custom-made, they were cut to fit the exact lines of the saddle skirts, most of which were of the round type.

Straight up
and scratching.

JO MORA

Stock saddles run in weight from the extra light ones, seldom under 25 pounds, up to 40 pounds or better. These weights, of course, without tapaderos. I've had plenty of arguments with horsemen of the English school of riding over the weights of our saddles. Most of these dudes had never seen cowboys working big stock and knew nothing about the ways of the Western ranges. Most claimed it was nothing short of cruel and barbaric to work a pony hard all day while packing a forty pound, or better, saddle besides the rider. Of course you can't argue with that kind of fanatic, but you can offer to bet a poke full of pesos that if he'll fasten a lass rope somehow or other through the pommel of his postage stamp and loop the other end over the horns of about 1,000 pounds of mad range bull, the ready answer will convince him who takes the stakes.

Now the cowboy's spurs. Just as in the matter of saddle riggings, bits, chaps, etc., the styles in spurs followed the same broad classification: one type for those from Texas and the ranges east of the Rockies, and another for those from the Pacific slopes. In a general way the latter were a trifle larger and silver-mounted, while the former lacked much of the ornament. Although spurs resemble each other considerably, to the practiced eye it was very easy to tell the difference between them, even with those of somewhat similar designs. In recent years, however, sectional characteristics are slowly giving way, and new designs are being developed and put on the market by the hundreds. As a rule, the old-type spur had buttons at the ends of the heel band to take the straps, and right below a slot to take the tie-down. Some of the new designs have all kinds of offsets and take-off angles to the strap buttons, and schemes for the tie-downs are many and varied, and some of them mighty good. They are even making bronc spurs with the shanks turned in so that a twister does not have to point his toes out when he wants to tickle or persuade his little pet.

However, a spur is a spur, after all, and has to have a heel band, a shank, a rowel, and some kind of gadget with which to tie it on. The old California spur had two chain loops hanging from a slot right under the strap button. One of these loops was longer than the other, and they were worn loose; that is, not fitting tight and snug to the arch of the boot. They were all right for a man in the saddle, but, for an ambling biped, they were no great help. Anyhow, when a California vaquero dismounted for any length of time, he generally took his spurs off; though it was not that way in many of the other ranges.

When I was riding in Arizona and New Mexico I used a spur that was quite popular there at that time. It was a plain, unadorned, short straight shank and a four-point rowel. The spur was tightly strapped to the boot (into which we tucked our overalls) and was not removed. When we'd take the boots off at night, the spurs stayed with them. Personally I like tight spurs, though I do like the style of the old California spurs (and I've worn one pair now for over 35 years), but I discarded the chains and use a tight strap to the arch.

The shanks on spurs are either straight, or ⅛, ¼, ½, or full curve, pointing down. They also made one that turned up and then broke down, but I don't think this was a very popular model. The conventional shank is generally made with a hook or guard on it, the best ones with a knob on this. This is called the chap guard. I see some of the ultra fancy modern ones have a little rowel set in this guard, just to make them fancier and trickier.

The old-time rowels were quite varied, running from as low as three points to about twenty. Some were cut in long, some short, and some were like a disc with serrated edge. They were of varied diameters, though not often going over three inches. The points were generally blunt. Modern rowels, however, run riot in shapes, and almost anything goes that will whirl, from points to serrations, to forked teeth, to flowers, etc. Sometimes, both in the old and new types, they may have a couple of little jinglers hanging from the outside rowel hub heads.

111

I realized that the sky's the limit these days with our prosperous movie waddies, when I looked through the catalogue of a house that caters quite exclusively to the Hollywood actors, hoi poloi, and the movie cowboys, and was interested in a picture and description of a pair of spurs and straps they had made for Tom Mix. They were overlaid in sterling silver with the heavy ornamentation of solid gold. Poor Tom must have been slipping at the time, because I read they had only been able to nick him for $650.00 for the spurs, and $245.00 for the straps. Oh, well, a waddie can't always be flush.

A little over thirty years ago, the boys held a rodeo show at San José, California. At that time, Timmy Sullivan, who was then a fine little bronc rider, owned a pet bull that he led around by a rope snapped to a ring in his nose. That bull was perfectly gentle and well mannered, and you could saddle him like any old livery crowbait. But—and here's where he displayed his masculine independence—just let a stranger crawl that hurricane deck, and the show that resulted was without a peer. With the saddle cinched well back over his loins, that long willowy body could whip up a buck that just could not be ridden by mortal cowboy, straight up and scratching. There was a standing offer of $50.00 for anyone who could stay with him under those conditions for fifteen seconds. Well, of course, Timmy brought the bull to the show, and there he stood saddled, hitched to the rail and dozing in bovine boredom.

It happened that to this show there drifted a colored boy who considered himself some rider and who was trying to break into the money scratching the bad ones at the shows which were fewer and farther between in those days than they are now. However, you also had to have entrance money to get into the events then at the professional shows, and I think that Mr. Howard Levey (which, by the way, was his name) found himself at that moment in a bit of a jam concerning his temporary bank rating with the big clearing houses. In other words he must have been broke; and, I imagine, in a desperate move to bolster his finances and assure himself the evening's pork chops after the show, he decided on a bold coup. He announced that he'd ride that bull of Timmy's if the $50.00 standing offer held good.

Well, that ambitious colored gentleman was very promptly assured that the offer did hold good, and the coming event was announced to the audience. Then the tentative hero asked if he might borrow a good pair of spurs for the séance, as it was his intention to scratch that bull plenty and no foolin'. Timmy asked me if I would loan him mine. This I did and he proceeded to strap them on tight, which was not easy as he was not wearing cowboy boots, but instead a pair of stiff, coarse brogans. Then, too, his foot did not have the genteel proportions of a prima donna's. But we finally got the job done and they were on as tight and rigid as could be.

The black boy now eased into the saddle and when Timmy unsnapped the rope from the ring in the bull's nose, he drove his heels into that cinch and worked around for a tangle hold. The fireworks started! Down went that bull's head and that famous willowy, whip-like buck began. Ordinarily, six or seven jumps was about all a human could sit, but this dusky lad was sho' nuf making a ride of it and whooping at every jump. The audience rose to its hind legs in puzzled expectancy, guessing at the seconds as the time passed, for it was like a butterfly riding the lash end of a mule skinner's whip. Everybody was pulling for him when a low groan ran through the crowd. He was loosening. He reeled to one side, yet was not thrown; the next buck jolted him back into the saddle; the next one loosened him again, and then he lost hold for good, and by all reckoning he should have been in the stratosphere preparing for his descent to terra firma. Yet his right leg stuck close to the bull's barrel, and like it was a pivot, he was jerked around till he faced the rear, his left leg swinging a grand arc over the saddle horn, and then he shot out sideways and hit the turf in a slide. He

113

seemed unhurt as he sat up, clowning a bit and shaking his fist at the bull who now had quit bucking and was jogging back to the rail. The crowd gave him a big hand as he stood up, scratched his wool, and started back for the stands with a slight limp. Then a roar went up: his right foot was unshod, and his brogan was dangling from the bull's belly, held there by the spur tangled in the strands of that hair cinch.

Although not straight up riding, he had smartly fished for that cinch, caught it properly with both spurs, and was making a showy ride of it when the left one let go, while the right one held and could not be loosened. Something had to give: the cinch wouldn't, the spur wouldn't, the ankle wouldn't, so that foot was positively jerked right out of its brogan! And when we untangled that rowel from the cinch, we found the spur shank had been bent in the argument. I have never had it straightened out, and I ride those same spurs to this day. But when the going gets tough and the bill collectors cut my trail too close for any fun, I can look at that spur and it's always good for a laugh.

Some sentimentalists, some who know nothing about horses, and, also, some who do, are violent opponents of the use of spurs. I'll not go into the merits of the argument, or the pros and cons to any great extent, but I will say that most of these opponents overlook the fact that the cowboy works at a very hazardous profession, much of the time on unbroken and half-broken horses; and that many of the situations he finds himself in during the course of a day's work demand instant and speedy action on the part of his mount; either to accomplish the job on hand, or in matters of life or death. Well, a pony should be broken to know that the rider wears a pair of hell rousers on his heels that can sure 'nuf make one squirm. Now it's up to the rider to know how to use them. Don't let the horse get hardened to them after the first few lessons. Just keep that accelerating power in reserve, and you can really "talk" to a well spur-broken horse by the pressure of your lower legs and the *suggested* action of your heels; or the real action with a light

114

touch, a harder one, or a smart jab according to the results required. A good, fairly blunt set of rowels, and I don't care how big they may be, are *not* cruel unless brutally used. It is true that I have seen abuses of spurs, and I've seen hard, ruthless riders fetch paint on their pony's flanks. But that's no indictment on the use of spurs. Far from it! Just take up your morning papers and it's a good bet you'll not have to look far before you find where some citizen has thoroughly beaten up his wife, decorated both her eyes, and forced her to seek the sanctuary of the Court for protection. Now then, we'll admit that's a tough break for the lady; yet it's scarcely an indictment on Marriage, or a sound enough reason for its abolishment, is it? Well, it's the same about spurs. Don't get maudlin or oversentimental about them for they are all right when they are used right, especially the cowboy's spur. And they can stand even a fair amount of ignorant use before they get real bad.

Spurs seem to be my fountain source for laughs, anyhow. I just told you of the way that dusky rider had bent my spur shank and the laugh I can always get out of the thought of that incident. Well, I can also get as good a laugh out of a comical situation anent another pair of my spurs. This was back in the days when Arizona was still a Territory. Three of us were riding from Flagstaff to St. Johns to fetch back a cavvy of Mormon horses. In passing through Winslow we decided we'd have the thrill of a real "boughten dinner." So we dismounted and went into the Harvey House at the depot to satisfy our cravings. After our meal, and perfectly satisfied with life, we propped the station wall and decided to wait for the Overland to roll in (we could hear it already tooting far down the line), and see what its herd of tourists had to offer in the line of human mavericks and strays.

Well, when the train finally ground to a stop and the porters cleared the doorways, that crowd just poured out and headed for the bell ringer at the hashery door so fast you could hardly tell the longhorns from the short. So we whiled away part of the time talking to the brakeman whom one of us knew. It didn't take long for that hungry bunch to gulp their bait. Before long, they commenced dribbling out, juggling toothpicks with their tongues, and looking around for something new to see in that remote corner of the Wild West. Most of them passed by us with but a casual glance at our overalls tucked into our spurred boots.

But pretty soon, a little bunch of six or seven men and women came out of the dining room, laughing, cackling, joking, and altogether good-naturedly noisy. A little, old lady, bespectacled, sharp-nosed and assertive, was the busiest, jokingest, and noisiest of the lot. She just knew she was comical, and you could tell in a flash she was "the real life of the party": yet I'll bet she topped 70 if she topped a day.

They were passing us in a noisy cackle, when one of the younger women spotted us, and, dropping her voice, we could hear in a stage whisper, "Oh, look over there at the cowboys." The old lady wheeled around, suddenly silent, and looked at us critically in a fast, all-comprehensive survey from the top of our sombreros to the high heels on our boots. Then she planted herself before me, hands on hips, and snorted, "Cowboys! Huh! What do you mean, young man, with those torturing hooks on your boot heels? Why, you cruel young savage . . . you, you . . ."

Well, I thought this unquestioned humorist was leading up to say something funny, but she just sputtered herself into a powerful heat, and the verbal dressing down she gave me for wearing spurs was nothing you could sneeze off. And it didn't help matters when one of my partners, who was quite a wag himself, broke in quietly and agreed with the old lady, and with a sad shake of his head confided that I had always been a hopeless case, and that my poor mother had never been able to do anything with me, anyhow.

Of course, everybody had gathered around by that time, and though the majority got a great laugh out of the proceedings, there were a couple who volunteered, in loud words, that the lady was right, after

116

all. When the conductor called "All aboard!", one of the boys gave a real ear-splitting war whoop, and the tourist herd poured back into the cars. As luck would have it, our persecutress sat down at a window quite in view of us, and as the train slowly pulled out and she passed us, we very politely took our hats off and wafted her a kiss. And I'll say right here that what she did then proved she was regular: she wafted one back to us with both hands!

Time and again I am asked whom I consider the better rider—the old-timer or the modern? And right here let me state for once and for all that this question is too much for me to answer. The truth is that I fail to see where a just, fair comparison can be made with conditions so different, especially in the matter of saddle types and horses. I've always tried to be an impartial observer throughout all these years, no matter what my personal likes and dislikes might have been. I'm certainly not one of those mossy horns who think that everything to do with "the good old days" was better than the modern. Far from it! I started out operating in the ways of the old school, and gradually I've eased into and have been a part of the modern evolution. I've seen the old-time cowboy astride a pony pass out with the longhorn and the great open ranges. Barbed wire, thoroughbred cattle, blooded horses, swell under-cut forks and shorter stirrups I've seen come and squat permanently. The only comparison I can make is that the old-timers, with their slick forks and long stirrups, had an unquestionably harder problem to keep glued to the hurricane deck on a volcanic bronc. That wide, swelled fork with *back bulges* and *undercut* heavily, the shorter stirrups raking forward, and the deeply dished cantle all tend to give a twister a seat that's as tight as that of a Knight in a tilting harness. It doesn't take one of particularly keen mentality—just half normal will do—to realize that there's no comparison possible as far as the saddle advantages go. The moderns have the edge. Well, you'd scarcely call it an edge; it's plain 100% advantage.

Wearing his "fish" in a squall.

Now then, on the other hand, possibly the riding of bigger, heavier, naturally stronger broncs makes a great difference on the other side of the scales. Now whether that equalizes the advantage in saddles, I really can't say. Who can? However, I will say that we "rassled" broncs of the mustang size, at least I did, with more disregard than we do today with the bigger hotblooded horses. Two of us, with few exceptions, could handle a pony bronc on foot, in many different ways. The commonest was to hobble the front feet, or trice up a back one, then slap on a blind and ear them down while the saddle was eased on and cinched. Now mind you, it wasn't always as easy as this all sounds; there were times, and plenty of them, when we'd tackle rowdies, tigers, and man eaters, and then we'd often have to call in the police. But, in general, we could wrestle them and get the job done handily. Yet I wouldn't try to ear down a 16 hand, 1200 pound part thoroughbred bronc. There are those that might, but I'm not one of that courageous breed and never have been. To the reader who does not know what "earing down" means, let me clarify. In this operation, a twister reaches either over or under the horse's head for his off ear, and grabs it with his right hand, while he likewise fastens to the near one with his left. Then he holds down as tight as he can, crowding in and trying to make himself as unshakable a part of that horse's head as possible. If the argument gets too rough, as it generally does, he can raise his body up by those ears, giving the bronc the job of holding that much dead weight by his neck. In many cases, some twisters also fasten on to the near ear with their own teeth to hold themselves closer and become more unshakable. This gentle, cute little operation is called "earing down," and sometimes in carrying it out, the man is dragged around like a puppy on a root, though his whole weight be pendant from those bronc ears.

Mustangs might have been quicker and snakier, but I do think that a big bronc may buck harder, you might say heavier, than a small one. So, in that respect, I'd give the disadvantage to the modern boys. Take, for instance, a big twelve- or thirteen-hundred-pound bronco that's a "pile driver"; the kind that go straight up and come down on all fours stiff-legged at one time. This type of bucker is not hard to stick from the standpoint of action, but the punishment he can deal to the rider is plenty, and can jar loose the moorings of your spine from the base of your skull. I may be prejudiced against this type, for it was just one of these bad actors that jarred me loose from too much conceit of getting to be a top bronc rider. The truth is that I started out too well on medium performers, and possibly was getting a little of that cockiness kids generally assume when they take dangerous chances and make good, and the older birds pat them on the back and sic 'em on.

I was with a little outfit that was picking up good, young cutting ponies from the ranches, or anywhere we could find them, and shipping them back East to be made into polo ponies. Most of our polo was played, in those days, on this type of pony and was an entirely different game from what it is today where those grand thoroughbreds come smoking down over the turf at race-track speed, and then take up half the field and part of the next county to turn and head back. Not so the old game. There, the little fellows played it plenty fast, too, but just like they learned it on the cutting grounds of the roundups and rodeos. They'd jam the breeze wide open, slide on their tails for a sudden stop, and wheel back with a spin that would unhorse you if you didn't ride every second of it.

We were camped, at the time, a few miles on the outskirts of San Antonio, Texas, and had turned over some stock to the Tappan Back Bay ranch, if I remember the name correctly after all these many years. At supper time another outfit of horse gyps drifted in and camped near us. They had some good-looking ponies, too, and, as you might expect, trading soon started up. The next day was Sunday and we both laid over, being joined by still another outfit. Of course trading kept up and quite a little drinking, and in the early afternoon we got up a couple of horse races between the best ponies from the different outfits. Considerable money changed hands. Then one thing led to another, and before I knew what it was all about, I had been matched to ride a bucking horse from the last outfit that joined us. The simple, yet severe conditions, were to ride straight up and scratch till the horse stopped bucking.

120

Busters of the 80's earing down and forking a bronco.

JO MORA

Well, they soon led out a very tall, big boned, hammer-headed black that would easily tip over 1200 pounds. He had collar scars on both shoulders, and small sunken eyes. This was certainly no saddle horse, for nobody rode such a moose in those days. He had us guessing, sure enough. But he led out as gentle as a schoolmarm's pet, and the halter rope was turned over to us. My helpers put on a coarse breaking hackamore with theodore that we had, with a common cotton rope, not a hair mecate, for reins. They had considerable adjusting to do to get that rig to properly fit that big head, and then my saddle was cinched on tightly. Considerable time was taken up with all this, and the boys worked with all due caution and ready for anything from this puzzling prospect. Yet there was never the slightest shake of the head or flattening of the ears; or humping of the back; or switching of the tail. I'll repeat that he had us guessing, for there was quite a little money posted on the result, and this big brute didn't act like a top-string bucker.

Then I eased up and into the saddle, settled myself, and gave the word to turn him loose. He never made a move. "Give 'im the gut hooks, cowboy," one of his owners drawled. I socked the rowels generously into his ribs in response, and the big black suddenly came to life and started off on a fast, heavy trot. I don't know how long he would have kept this up, but I felt the showdown would have to come sooner or later, so why delay? I jabbed him in the shoulder and raked back heavily to his loins, and he broke then into a run from which, without any further persuasion or warning, he went up into the air higher than I ever dreamed a big coarse plug like that could go; and when he returned to terra firma his four legs stiffened and he came down on them all at one time. This procedure, the fast run and the high stiff-legged buck jump, he repeated again, and again, and again. He was not hard to ride, but the punishment he dealt when he landed was terrific. After a dozen or more jolts, I really thought I was going to faint and I came within an ace of letting go and "abandoning ship." It was just kid pride that made me hold out, for my actions were getting purely mechanical with my brain in such a cockeyed whirl.

I don't know what the inspiration was, but it suddenly flashed in my befuddled brain to get his head around, and with all my weight and strength I jerked his nose around roughly when he raised his head for his short runs. I almost laid his muzzle on my knee, and for a moment I felt sure we were going down in a tangle. He staggered ahead wildly and finally regained his feet. Before he could get his head down again, I whirled him once more, and he broke into a trot and whinnied himself back to his own cavvy.

When I swung off, my knees would scarcely hold me up, though it was mostly mental for I couldn't see straight, feeling as dizzy as if I'd been swung around in a whirl. I had won in the gamble, but I had more of the bronc-riding conceit shaken out of me than if I'd had a dozen spills. I knew, way down deep, that I wasn't built to stand much more of that type of heavy hammering, and that a steady diet of such would eventually land me in the funny factory. I tried to act nonchalantly, but what I did get was a good-natured laugh all around, for I staggered off, weaving unsteadily with my hands out in front of me like I was walking in the dark. I was just "punch drunk" for a short spell, that's all. Yet for several years after this incident I hoped that sunken-eyed black had found his proper niche in the glue works. I've been piled by broncs and "gentle horses" since, but I've never been hurt like I was by that plug that day.

So I guess I'll have to vote that the modern, bigger, hot-bloods are tougher to ride. This may even up advantages in saddles, or it may not. Who can say? Anyhow, this I do know: a GOOD rough rider is GOOD no matter what the conditions are; and the old-timers could have scratched them just that much easier in the modern bronc saddles, and the modern peelers should have done just as well in the old days with slick forks on smaller broncs. Anyhow, those are my sincere convictions. One was just as good as the other, for they are all the same breed, and why waste a lot of hot air trying to prove the impossible?

In the matter of everyday, common-ordinary style in the saddle, I think the old-timers were possibly a shade the more graceful and picturesque riders. They rode with a long stirrup, an exceedingly long one in some localities, and the torso set straighter from the saddle, almost a straight line (in profile) from head to heel. Their only creed was to keep the bosom of their pants glued to that saddle seat and show no daylight under any conditions or gaits. If, for some reason, you had to ride a trot for a way, and that trot was rough and heavy, you just rode it anyhow, glued right there and not the slightest rising in the stirrups or the faintest hint at posting. That was only made for dudes and Englishmen —it was taboo on the range.

The modern boys, however, are not so fussy about this, because, with the shorter stirrup, the seat has changed a trifle. You will see, these days, on the cutting grounds or among the pickup men at the shows, that some of them, between chores when their horses trot a little in taking a new stand, may be inclined to rise in their stirrups to avoid the joggle of the trot. Another position many affect these days while jogging, is to rise a little and rest on the stiffened arms with the hands cupped over the horn. There's nothing wrong with this, and most of these riders are tip-top, A-1 cowboys, but from the standpoint of handsome cowboy riding, they just look like hell to me.

IV

nyhow, *let's* drift into something where there's no argument possible, and that is that you can't be a cowboy
without cows. So, let's take a little pasear, if only in
mental leaps, and see what kind of cow critters the
first cowboys messed around with. And that's where we
ride slap-bang into the Texas Longhorn, the old Spanish Cow of history
and legend, the Coaster, the Sea Lion, the Cactus Boomer, the Mossy
Horn: all one and the same except as to their native range and age.
Here he was, hammer-headed and onion-eyed, and packing a pair of
horns that were a sight to behold . . . often six feet and better across.
They were either of fine, curved, conventional types, or almost straight
across with a couple of corkscrew spirals that give him a very business-
like appearance for side thrusting, if not so hot for a head-on crash.
When a steer passed his 7th or 8th birthday, these horns took on a scaly
and crinkled texture, and readily earned the name they were given
. . . Mossy Horns. He was leggy, full of angles, and his chassis was
designed for endurance and speed, and was made up of hardened
muscles and tough, elastic tendons. Like the wild creature he was, he
had little time or inclination to accumulate fat with soft and tender
muscles. He was an individualist and lover of personal liberty, and for
this he was ready to fight any time and with mighty little coaxing. Yet,
when taken from his native mesquitales to the far northern ranges, he
readily took on a couple of hundred pounds. Even then, make no mistake about it, he was still the athlete.

There isn't one layman in a thousand who has any idea of the task the old time Texan stockmen had in putting up those vast herds they drove north over the long trails. As a matter of fact there are some modern stockmen that might also be included in that list. When one of these starts telling me how, in fairly recent years, he has had as ornery and spooky, and wild cows to work as any old longhorn, I just know that hombre doesn't begin to know what it's all about. Let me state right here that I, too, have had to work mean, touchy, wild cows, especially in rugged, heavily chaparaled hill country. I've worn down good ponies on these cusses, and I've been mad enough to cry on some of these chores, yet I know the worst of it was kindergarten stuff compared to what the boys had to contend with when putting up a herd of those spooky hellions from the brasadas of southwest Texas, in the early days.

Personally, I was born a little too late in the century to have had a chance to work with the genuine old Texas Longhorns. Things moved so fast in the cattle industry when the reign of the Cowboy commenced after the Civil War, that a short space of time, like ten or twenty years, could create a change that seems unbelievable. When I was born, the longhorns were at the peak of their popularity on the great trails, and yet, twenty years later, when I threaded their ranges in the saddle, they had already been superseded by a different-looking cow. Bovine styles were then for shorter horns, and the rangy, fast, old mossy horn had given way to a critter that could pack more tender beef and fat and hold it. I've seen and sketched many a longhorn, but I never had the chance to work them on the open range. They were, even then, "live museum specimens," the same as the Buffalo they had crowded off those same ranges but a very few years before. However, they had served their usefulness, but there was more money in the new type, and that's all that counted. The longhorn had just been a pawn of commerce; and there's small sentiment in commerce. And, as for that, why should there be? At best, he was a tough, scrappy specimen,

126

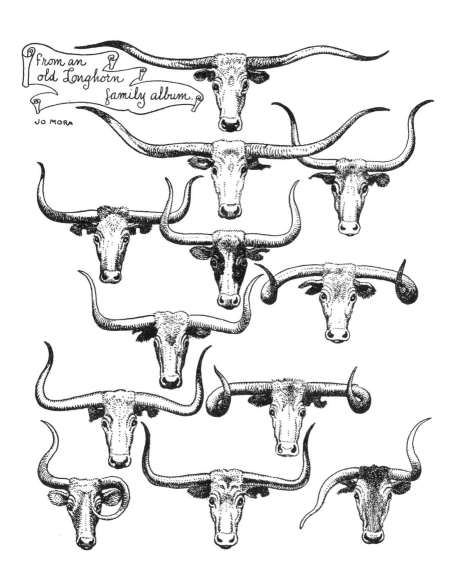

from an
old Longhorn
family album.

JO MORA

mighty picturesque though, I'll admit, and it isn't hard to work up plenty of romance from such a type. The same as we do with so many of our colorful badmen who were, after all, nothing but rats. So, when the showdown comes, we'll string along where the dividends are high and the danger slight.

However, if I did just miss intimate association and knowledge of this same old Mossy Horn, I certainly had the advantage of hearing and discussing, first handed, the characteristics of this bovine individualist with cowboys who, but a very few years past, had worked and known no other type of cow. So recent were their experiences, and so exciting their anecdotes, that I absorbed it all to that point where, as the years rolled by, I almost thought I had been through those longhorn days myself.

Let's take a clear look at that picture. As I have stated before, after the Civil War, Texas found itself teeming with uncounted thousands of longhorned cows. They were worth in the market but a few dollars a head and with mighty few buyers. There was no incentive to run the stock business on an efficient, economical basis. There were countless old mavericks (unbranded cattle) roaming the brush that had never felt the tickle of a rope on their anatomies, and who lived and died there in that blissful state of freedom. The Texas range is diversified, but there's a big chunk of it in the southern part that's about as thick and pesky a piece of brushland as God Almighty ever spread out for humans to cuss over. I refer to the Mesquitales of south Texas: and there, gentle reader, is brush what am BRUSH! Please take this from one who has been there.

Of course, the rougher and thicker the cover, the more protection for the wild game living in it; and by this natural law, there was the happy hunting ground of Mr. and Mrs. Tex Longhorn. There they were, plenty of them: now, how in heck to get them out and drive them away to market and stick to the conventions of law and order. Well, I'll tell

A couple of mossy horns

Texas Longhorns

JO MORA

you what it was like: it was just like someone had given you the contract to put up a herd of so many hundred wild deer and deliver them,
by their own locomotion, to some spot a thousand miles away.

Cows can certainly be pesky critters when they get inclined that
way, as every stockman who has ever had to work range cattle can
testify, but I've seldom met up with one that could not be turned by
a good rider on a good horse. In this I except cows that temporarily go
on the prod after you get them out of a mire hole, or some mean old
bull that gets too hot and bothered and stubborn. These, and other
similar cases, I except, though they too can be handled if you savvy
cows and use cow diplomacy.

But that was not the case with the majority of the old mossy horns
of the early southern Texas ranges. When one of those ladinos came
to the realization that you were interfering with his constitutional

rights he just started for somewhere and did not care a damn who or what stood in the way, be it man, horse, both or whatnot. He just kept on going, with red in his eye and a will to prove that those all-embracing horns had not been planted on his poll to grow only into a record trophy for the dude's den. Oh, yes, he'd run from trouble every chance he got; but when trouble headed him off and he resolved to go on the prod, no mounted man could turn him unless he stood him on his head with a tailing; or he roped and busted him; or he shot him through the horns; or he just killed him. He'd stop for nothing else, and SPCA methods never could alter that set-up.

In the bayou and lake ranges of the coast, when hard pressed, those cows would deliberately make for water and take to it like a bunch of hell divers, and they were just as much at home in the wet as they were on land popping the brush. They didn't dive in because they were herded there; they took to it with malice aforethought, knowing every inch of the terrain, and the depth of a water hazard or the distance to the next bit of terra firma meant positively nothing to them. Could they swim! Now, if you think those "sea lions" and "coasters" were easy to work in that kind of country, I'd like to know what you really call tough.

Most of those old longhorns had been free and unhandled by man for so long that they were turned into real wild animals. Not domestic animals gone wild, but honest to hokey wild game. Many of them, like deer, kept to the heavy brush throughout the day; and please believe me when I state once more that by brush I mean BRUSH— nothing more and nothing less. It really seemed almost impenetrable. There's still plenty of it left, I'm told, so go down there and look it over if you are skeptical. And how those leggy, spooky critters could bust through it at top speed while packing maybe a six-foot spread of horns, is, to me, one of the unsolved mysteries of all times. The real, wild bunch stayed in the cover all day and came out only at dark to feed on the prairie grass. To flush out of that cover, and to round up a

Old time Tejano tailing a mossy horn.

Jo Mora

bunch of those outlaws in the daytime, was a difficult, specialized, dangerous job that took men and horses highly trained in a peculiar technique that called for guts, dash, absolute disregard for danger and death. Dogs, too, were often used in this work.

Let's say, for the sake of the picture, that we've flushed a bunch of of the wild ones out of that brush and into the open . . . what then was the next move? Could you herd them together and drive them along in more or less the direction to camp? A certain percentage might have enough of the herd instinct, though wild as deer, to allow themselves to be driven in a given direction by dint of very hard riding on the part of the herders. Yet a great part of them would go just so far and then they'd break out and high-tail it for the brush. The chances are that the runaway could not be readily headed and turned in time, if at all, so the next recourse was to give it a "coleo" (a tailing) and stand

131

it on its head to come down with a thump that would knock the wind out of it completely and even possibly break a horn, a rib, or a neck sometimes. It was not gentle medicine: but neither was running long-horns a gentle game. In most cases the potent dose worked, and when that surprised, windless, bruised bovine gangster got to his feet unsteadily, he might temporarily be a "good boy" and fall in with the moving herd and give no further trouble. However, after a hard tailing, an old ladino might just sulk and stubbornly refuse to budge an inch from his recumbent position in spite of all the persuasions, all the expedients, rough, painful, yes, very often cruel. But this was a hard game and a dangerous one. Tail twistings, six-shooter shots close to tender parts, dirt in the eyes, hard spurrings, lashings with the quirt or coiled lariat, draggings with a rope and horse, in fact everything that a desperate cowboy could think of, often failed.

Sometimes one of those expedients would work, and then up would pop that red-eyed hellion "on the prod." Then it was gangway, everybody! In that frame of mind a mad mossyhorn would never listen to reason, and another tailing or a rope busting was all that could be done. However, as I have stated, there were those that nothing could induce to get up short of dynamite or a derrick. In that case, if the subject was some snipe-gutted old outlaw that wasn't worth six bits as prime beef and was known to be a bad moral influence on the little doggies of that neighborhood, it's an even bet he'd be planted there with a lead slug between the eyes to furnish comfort for coyotes and buzzards. And good riddance it might be, too, for a real trouble maker could mess up things scandalously; and those hard-worked vaqueros had trouble enough even when things were going along at an average tempo.

Another way to control bad breakaways that could not be readily headed back into the bunch was for the nearest vaquero to take down his string, though it's a good chance he already had it coiled in his hand and was slapping his leggings with it, and drape a loop over that critter's horns and then try to lead him or drive him ahead aided by others

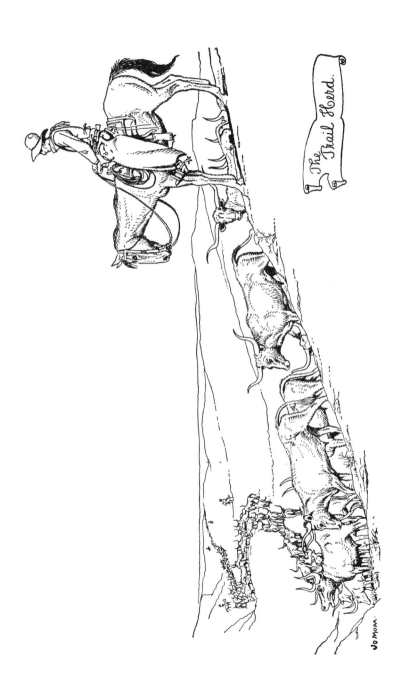

The Trail Herd.

to keep him going in the right direction. Sometimes this worked; and then again it didn't. So, with all the pesky outlaws that could not be herded along, they generally tied them up to a tree, or gave them a tumble and hog-tied them with a piggin' string to stay out there all night to think it over and cool off. Most of those outfits had trained oxen that they'd drive out, in the morning, to where the bad ones had been left. These would then be necked (lashed together by the necks) to the gentle stock, and the pair would worry along back to camp herded by a rider. There were also some of these gentle oxen that could be turned loose with their "prisoners" and they would find their own way slowly back to camp.

Many years ago, in the Apache country of southern Arizona, I heard the following story at a C C C ("cherry cow") campfire. The teller was an old waddie who had been born in Webb County, Texas, when the brasada along the Rio Grande was the real training ground for so many of the boys that went up the long trails with the longhorns in the 70's. He said he was riding with a crowd of neighboring ranchmen who were contracted to furnish part of a big herd that was to go up the trail to Abilene. They were working out the mesquitales on their home ranges, and the cows were mighty wild and brush fighters for keeps. They had a good herd of gentle stock for decoys and several dependable oxen that were trained to bring in their outlaws when the occasions demanded. One of these, he said, was a big savino veteran of many a campaign, who had lost an eye in the service of his calling. He stated it seemed there was nothing in the line of ornery, fighting longhorn that El Tuerto * couldn't cope with and bring into camp unaided. He also declared that there was on that same range a big, long-legged, snipe-gutted maverick red steer that had been seen and run in the brush by many of those ranchers for several years; yet not one of them had ever been able to work it out into the open or dab a rope on it. This steer got

* The one-eyed.

134

to be quite a mystery and was looked upon, in that locality, almost like a ghost or something unnatural. The fact that he was a steer and a maverick made it all the more mysterious, for when a bull calf is castrated to be turned into a steer, he generally acquires a brand at the same time. But this ladino's red hide showed not a trace of a running iron. Several of the ranchers had come within an ace of taking a shot at him when seen in the brush, but the very mystery that time wove about him kept them from pulling trigger. Everybody reckoned he'd live to die a natural death of old age right there in his native brush, though some of the more imaginative wouldn't have been surprised to see him stay there forever as a bovine "ha'nt." He was known as Ole Red.

Then something happened in quite an unexpected manner. The crowd had decided to work out one section of that range by the light of a full moon, and were lucky enough to sneak up on a good-sized bunch that were feeding out far enough from cover for the riders to race in between and cut them off. Every waddie had his rope whirling and, when pandemonium broke loose, the bewildered cows dashed here and there while the hissing loops were finding their marks. But few casts were lost. Then came the fun of busting and hog-tying, and things moved fast for many minutes.

One vaquero had spilled his loop over the horns of a big steer just as it dashed into the brush, and the cover was too thick for the rider to bust him. In the struggle that followed, horse, rider, and steer got pretty well tangled up. Then, of a sudden, that steer turned and charged. The Lord was looking out for that waddie that night, for the infuriated steer went around a tree when it turned to attack, and fetched up at the end of the rope a scant yard in front of the pony which had been reined up sharply. The steer's head jerked back at the violent snub, yet so determined was his forward speed that his body swung right around, completely turning tail and side-swiping the pony with a force that took him off his feet, the rider still in the saddle. The situation was serious enough, yet plenty humorous, for the pony over-lapped that steer by almost half his length, and the rider reached down and grabbed its tail as the maddened captive kicked furiously.

There was little the vaquero could do but call for help, and before long two of the boys rode up, one who had already tied his critter, and another who had wasted his loop. They dabbed their ropes on that steer's horns, and then the first rider loosened his string from the saddle horn and cast it loose. They had no easy job dragging that scrapper out of the brush and into the open, but when they got out there they dis-covered, by the light of that full moon, that they had snared Ole Red "hisself."

With three ropes on him they started to lead him along, when he must have realized that all his fighting was to no avail, for he just threw himself, and then nothing they could do would make him get up on his feet. So they hog-tied him, and left him there, with the rest of his cap-tive bunch, to await the morning hours and the oxen. Of course, they picked El Tuerto to bring Ole Red into camp; and though the latter had been hog-tied all night, his fighting spirit was not one bit dulled, and they had a real tussle to neck those two together. Then they left them to work out their own traveling schedule and routine.

Nobody worried about El Tuerto when he didn't show up the next morning, for it generally took that length of time, and often longer, for such combinations to plod back to camp. In fact, they didn't even think much of it when they failed to put in an appearance the morning after that. They all figured that things were going tougher than of an average but as El Tuerto had never yet "failed to bring in his man," nobody seemed to get unduly excited over it. However, on the morning of the third day the outfit was changing hunting grounds and moving to a new range and corrals about fifteen miles away; and when those absentees failed to show up, a couple of the boys were delegated to stay behind and ride back to find out what had happened.

Well, they cut their tracks a half mile or so from where they had last been seen, and by the nature of the evidence they found graved in that soil, there was no doubt that the battle had been spirited. The tracks led back gradually, though somewhat zigzaggedly, towards the brush and finally entered it. Then for a stretch it continued into it deeper and deeper. Then it curved out again toward the open, leaving a trail that resembled the path of a road crew laying out a boulevard. The trackers stopped several times to listen, for if that battle was still raging it should have been heard, in that heavy brush, for a half mile or more. But they heard nothing.

Then, at last, right at the edge of the brush, they could see El Tuerto lying down seemingly at ease. The only movement visible was that of his ears as he turned them to catch the sounds of the approaching horsemen. His head was lowered so that the muzzle rested on the ground. There was Ole Red, necked to him, stretched out as stiff as a mackerel! Cold and rigid, he must have cashed in many hours before that. What a battle that must have been! Though this was late Spring, the heat had been very intense for several days (it does get hot there), and that infuriated ladino must have worked himself into the kind of a frenzy that pops them off very frequently in that country. The scorching sun will often melt a cow or a pony into the happy hunting grounds if greatly overtaxed.

Well, they freed the old veteran from his ex-sparring partner, and, after a long wait, he struggled wobblingly to his feet, yet seemed unable to walk. He had had no food or water for three whole days, struggling every minute in the stifling heat of that brush. There seemed to be nothing the boys could do about it, for the nearest water was several miles away, and they had nothing but their hats to fetch it in, so they wished the old-timer luck and rode away to overtake the outfit on the move to the new camp.

They reported their findings and, naturally, El Tuerto was the subject of campfire talk for the next couple of nights and his passing was deplored as that of a game old veteran who had met his match at last. Then, the next morning, when the decoys and the lead oxen were cut from the herd to do their appointed daily work, there was El Tuerto among them, as phlegmatic as ever, and seemingly none the worse for his recent championship battle. True, he hadn't brought in his man, but he had held him for the coroner. And then, instead of wandering back to his home corral, the old rascal had followed the outfit for fifteen miles to the new camp. A loyal veteran, sure enough.

Sometimes, with those ladinos that had been left overnight tied up, they'd drive the decoys among them when they loosened them, and it was a fair bet that they'd get up with a different viewpoint on life, at least for the time being, and drift along with the gentle ones. Yet imagine putting up a herd of a thousand or so under those circumstances. Do you get the picture? Well, this only gives you a hazy idea of the real hard, dangerous work it was to chouse those hellions out of that brasada and break them into the semblance of a trail herd. After getting a bunch out of the brush, and leaving the bad ones tied up on the ground, that remaining aggregation of onion-eyed, horning, fighting cows was closely herded along and driven to the camp. Now, don't think for a second that, once there, they were rounded up and bedded down for the night to be lulled to sleep by a couple of crooning cowhands. Not much! Had they tried this they would have had but a few cripples and a doggie calf or two to answer the morning roll call. That wild bunch had to be penned, and camps were always made near proper-sized and strong corrals. There that crazy bunch of "cactus boomers" was headed and gradually worked over to and into the corral gates.

Then came the job of getting them inside, and don't think it was easy. It took men that savvied cows to do that job, and, like as not, they might lose half, or more, of all they had gathered in the tiresome day's work. A crazy critter might put its head down and dash out like greased lightning, and if it couldn't be tailed right there, the riders would let it go, for if they left an unguarded spot for too long, where one got through, a dozen might follow. Anticipating all this trouble, from former experiences, they'd always try to arrive at the corrals not too late, so that they might have considerable daylight left, after the main bunch was corraled, to go after and try to bring back all those that had broken loose. Sometimes the boys didn't get back to their grub till long after dark. There were no Union hours in those days, though most of those cowmen were ranchers themselves, and a day's work was just as long as the job remained undone. Even after corraling, that job was not done. They had to keep a pretty good watch all night, for those spooky critters were just as liable as not to start a stampede right there inside that corral. If the bunch within was small and they had room enough to get under full steam for a frenzied run, few picket and rawhide corrals, as they were made in southern Texas, could stand the strain of that impact. And even if they didn't break through, the result of one of those wild, crazy "uprisings" left many a cripple and even dead ones for the morning clean-up,

All I can think of by way of comparison, is a little game we had, which was very popular when I was a kid, called "Pigs in Clover." I guess most of you are familiar with it. Remember trying to get those marbles into the center corral? When you'd tilt the board to "persuade" some marbles through one gate, those already penned would roll out through their gate. It was a great game, and though it could be done, it took patience and skill, and lots of both. Putting up a herd of longhorns reminds me of that game. But it was no parlor pastime; it was a particularly dangerous game. Casualties happened right along, and seldom a day passed in those cow hunts that some horse or rider wasn't crippled or gored, slightly or seriously, or even killed. It was a man's job, all right, and our later-day round-ups and rodeos with all their exhilarating thrills, and mishaps, and hazards, can in no way compare, from the standpoint of danger, with those early cow hunts in the mesquitales of southern Texas.

Even after that wild bunch had survived an uneventful night in the corral, they had to be day herded mighty gingerly that they might graze and drink and still show few a.w.o.l's. They would be let out early in the morning, and the whole outfit would guard them closely till they had quieted down completely, and then, little by little, the riders would slip away till only the regular day herders were left. These would watch them closely all day, and many a breakaway had to be tailed. They depended much on the gentle stock, decoys, and lead oxen to keep that bunch together, and it would take several days to break them to their new environment. Now, it would have been fine and dandy if their education had been allowed to proceed along normal lines, but you must realize that every evening a fresh bunch of snorting, scrapping, horning, wild recruits was added to their numbers. I don't think it takes much imagination to realize what these could do to mess up the decorum and herd manners the others had already absorbed. It was a continual turmoil right up to, and including, the road branding, the counting, and the first few days on the long trail. At the start, a great many extra vaqueros were used to help string out that bunch into trail formation, and to shove them along at a fast pace to really tire them out and get them as far away as possible from their home ranges. In those first few days they wanted those cows to be leg-weary when evening came so that they'd be better inclined to bed down quietly and forget their bad manners.

Barring the outlaws that always caused trouble on the trail, the majority of a herd could soon be broken into a regular, phlegmatic trail routine, with individual members dropping into their accustomed places, same leaders, same "soldiers" bringing up the rear. If the weather was good and the grass likewise, they'd really put on weight,

A ladino goes on the prod

JO MORA

idling along, grazing as they'd go, and covering from ten to fifteen miles a day. But if a drover did not get the breaks, and had to deal with things like bad thunderstorms to stampede his cows, freshets at the river fords, waterless drives, red and white human vultures, he might land at the trail's end with a decidedly slimmer herd than he started out with.

There were liable to be many bovine trouble makers and outlaws in a big herd, especially in the early ones, and they could certainly raise havoc with an outfit on the slightest provocation. After a stampede, those longhorns would be scattered over the landscape like seed from a broadcaster. Many an old ladino scalawag evaded the drag after such happenings, and found his way back to his native mesquital, there to be gathered up once more and schooled for another try over the long trail. Some of these inveterate trouble makers get to be well known, and many finally succumbed to an attack of lead poisoning, for cows were too cheap to fuss around with gangsters. All such should have been "tamed" at the very start: and it would have been vastly more economical in the end.

So, up the long trails went the longhorns, thousands on thousands of them, to the shipping points springing up on the westward advancing railroads. Then, with the extermination of the buffalo and the rounding up of the Indians, the great grazing lands of the North were thrown open with a boom for cattle the like of which this country had never known. So the longhorn populated those ranges, too, till Texas commenced to feel the drain on her reservoir of cows.

Well, ours was a new country; frontiers disappeared overnight; and the evolution progressed not by slow stages, but by leaps and bounds, like a magician pulling a mouse out of the hat, and then by a sudden presto-chango turning it into a rabbit. The longhorn was a pawn of commerce, and commerce must seek a profit in its transactions to exist. There was a time when herds were bought by numbers, on the hoof, and a cow was a cow, be it only a lean, tough, wrinkle-necked, old mossyhorn, or a prime four-year-old steer packing all the beef and fat one of his breed could. Yes, a cow was a cow. But all that soon changed. Buyers wanted to pay only for what they got in beef and suet, and it soon got to be a matter of pounds not numbers. The longhorn couldn't stand that competition. True, he'd take on considerable weight, for him, when transplanted to the grasses of those northern ranges, but even then the deck was stacked against him. "All horns and hair" didn't go any more with buyers.

Barbed wire also came into the picture about that time, and once the Texan could control his own brand, he commenced grading up his herd; and though everybody had his own ideas about that, I think it was the Durham and the Hereford that took the early lead in popularity for real beef results. So, curtains for the Longhorn! In true American style the change was sudden and complete. So long, old mossyhorn, you sho nuf did your stunt while you occupied the stage. Your act was short, but it was certainly picturesque, exciting, and American in every way. And I'll bet that if there are any longhorn ghosts floating over those vast stretches that were once the Long Trails, they must give many a spectral snort as they behold their white-faced, short-horned and muley successors, hand fed in the corn belt and waddling along in obese serenity.

The make-up and handling of a trail herd, though each outfit did it in its own way, held more or less to a similar pattern in average weather and terrain. The size of herds varied from several hundred to thousands. From two to four thousand were big herds. They went even as high as six thousand. However, after several years of trail driving, I think it was found much more expedient to take the smaller herds. They were easier to handle and more economical in the long run.

In the early days they were made up of stock from different brands, and all had to be road-branded for the trip; and the wagon boss had to pack around, close to his person, the various bills of sale that he might show at a moment's notice that everything was regular with his herd. Sometimes an owner took up his own herd, though, more often, it was put in charge of a foreman or wagon boss. The number of cowboys taken was quite flexible, according to the generosity or the tightness of the owner, just as in any other pursuit administered by humans. Some herds were undermanned; others quite the opposite. As the trail problems to be faced got better known, and there was not so much guessing to be done, things got down to more of a standard. You might say that two cowboys to every three hundred and fifty cows was a good average, each hand with a string of six or eight ponies. You must remember that these ponies were all grass-fed, and they could not have been ridden and worked continuously for three, four, or five months without plenty of rest and time to graze as they went along. The horse herd was called the cavvy or cavyard, western U. S. for "caballada," Spanish for horse herd. It was also called the remuda, which is Spanish for re-change or remount.

The cavvy was in charge of a horse-wrangler (a remudero) and good outfits had two; one for the day and another for the night. The latter was called the night-hawk. As each cowboy had to stand night watch for a certain number of hours, they generally staked out their saddled "night horses" where they might be readily reached when their round of duty arrived or for instant avail in case of stampede or other urgent necessity. These night horses were, of course, the quietest of the string, yet had to be also fast and sure-footed, for when they were needed in one of those terrific emergencies, they were *needed* and I don't mean maybe! Racing in front of a seething mass of frenzied longhorns dashing in delirious abandon over treacherous, rough ground in utter darkness (possibly in a thunderstorm) was no place to be riding a sprung-kneed veteran, unless quick suicide was the desired objective. A top night horse had to be good. If the outfit had no night-hawk, the cavvy was generally hobbled out at night.

144

And from the same family this stall-bred, hand-fed, Blue-ribboned gourmet's dream →

Can you vision this sissy on the long trail from the Gulf to the Black Hills? How times do change!

That A.1. modern range favorite the White Face.

Longhorn~ Alert. scrappy. trail-blazing Pioneer.

Buffalo~ The original~ Native Son.

The Evolution of Western North American Beef

JO MORA

Another important item of a trail herd was the chuck wagon. Early ones were often heavy, two-wheeled carts drawn by a couple, or more, yokes of oxen. Later, horse-drawn wagons were used entirely, being more mobile and faster. And with the chuck wagon went that most important autocrat of the outfit, the Trail Cook. He might be called the "old lady," or other names of similar regard, yet he held a position that could be, and generally was, very despotic according to the character of the individual. No matter what happened on the trail, the *cook was the cook!* The hard-working cowboys had to have the necessary "fuel" to keep up that required energy; and you couldn't get choosey and drift over to the corner delicatessen for a change of diet. You just took what the outfit cook prescribed, and he might be good, indifferent, or bad. Damned bad, sometimes! Vitamins had not as yet been invented, and a "balanced diet" on the long trails was quite unheard of. Don't think every bucaroo was the acme of virile health and bubbling exuberance. It is true that the hard, outdoor life took the edges off many parlor ills, but there was plenty of dyspepsia and heartburn in the saddle. And small wonder after the way those waddies bolted their bait before sun-up, washed it down with plenty of stout, black coffee, and then kept it thoroughly stirred by the constant jolting of an active, working pony. Scarcely the recipe for "sweet tummies."

Well, that just about takes in all the component parts of a trail outfit. Early in the a.m., long before sunrise, the cook's instinct, his alarm clock, or one of the last watch woke him up, and he busied himself with getting the breakfast ready. The great herd soon got up on its feet with a stretch or two, and the boys on watch quietly, and without any apparent effort at forcing them, got them headed in the direction of the planned day's drive; allowing them to graze at leisure yet always drifting in the desired direction. The rest of the boys would soon be up and bolting a bait, and the night-hawk would bring in the remuda, herding it over to the chuck wagon. Here some of the boys would surround it and form an improvised corral of human posts and rope rail. Cow ponies were taught to respect a rope early in their training and this method worked well, though I have seen times when bull-headed or half-broken ponies were not overly respectful. But slips will happen in the best-regulated drugstores, so the popular saying goes. Inside this rope corral, the boys moved around quietly, dragging their loops and snapping them over the heads of the ponies they'd pick out for the day's work. The night horses were then turned loose. The cowboys saddled up, mounted, and took over the herd from the night watch, who came in now, had their breakfast, and roped out fresh horses. Maybe they'd give the cook a hand hitching up the wagon team, picking up his paraphernalia and stowing away into the wagon any odds and ends, along with the bed rolls of the entire outfit. When all was in order, the cook would fall in behind the grazing herd, and the wrangler would bring up the rear with his cavyard. In this order, more or less, they would graze along, and, of course, wherever there was water the herd would be given its fill. And this matter of water was a very serious and all-important one to the drover. There were stretches on some of those trails where, in dry years, the problem of getting the great herds safely over them turned into tragedies or near-tragedies. Another one of those things to make the trail driver's lot not altogether one bed of roses. Just the thorns from them, I guess.

Later in the morning, according to the pasturage and general conditions, say about 9 o'clock, the herd would be strung out into more of a marching formation. A couple of the cowboys, one on each side, near the head of the column guided the movement and direction of the leaders. These were called the "point riders." On either side other cowboys rode controlling the main body and the flanks. These were the "swing riders." Those bringing up the rear were the "tail riders," and they had to ride herd on the footsore, the lame, the halt and the

TRAIL DUST AND SADDLE LEATHER

lazy. The leaders were "self appointed" and they'd generally keep their stations throughout the whole trip. In fact, this applies to most of the herd, its individual members taking up certain stations which they maintained permanently. The cowboys got to know their charges pretty well as they rode herd on them day after day, week after week, and a wise trail boss gradually weeded out the trouble makers, turning them into beef for the cook to juggle, or as "graft," or "toll fees" when they crossed the Nations and the demands of the Red Brothers got too hot. Anyhow, in this manner a herd would average its ten or fifteen miles a day, though the tempo could be greatly increased when it was necessary; just as it was often decreased by accidents or unfavorable incidents and conditions in the march.

At noon the herd would be allowed to graze again or lie down at leisure. The cook generally unlimbered sufficiently to give the boys a cold snack. Campfires were not as a rule built, though some cooks insisted on hot coffee. Much of the terrain traversed was treeless, except along the rivers and creeks, and the popular campfire fuel was "buffalo chips," the desiccated dung of buffaloes or cows. It made a good hot fire in dry weather, though when too wet it did not burn so readily, all of which scarcely added to the sweet temper or the efficiency of the cook. Under those conditions it also gave out a smudge odor—well, it wasn't exactly an odor either; it was just a God-awful stink which was no perfume for delicate nostrils. I guess many of us did not have delicate nostrils in those days; we just had smellers. At its best it gave out a pungent aroma, and I really think we got lonesome for it when away from it too long. To this day, in fancy, I can smell it, and my daydreams are of distant horizons and days in the saddle that will never return for me.

After the midday rest they would trail along once more and when they arrived at the bedding ground which had been previously selected, they were slowly stopped and allowed to graze and were watered, if such was there. Then, when the time came, they were bedded down for the night. Good cowboys, those who have real cow sense, can make a nice job of watering or bedding down a large herd; poor hands can make a mess of either, no matter how clever they might be at riding broncs or roping. It takes real cowboys to do those jobs. The bedded herd must be compact yet not crowded, for much might happen throughout the night. Then in the matter of watering a large, thirsty herd at a restricted water locality, that too is a job only for those who savvy cows. City clerks should not apply.

The cowboys of a trail herd, who generally slept in pairs, were divided into night watches which might be of from two to four hours' duration according to the number of riders in the outfit. While on guard they were mounted on their quietest and best ponies, their "night horses," and as they made their monotonous rounds they sang and crooned the while. Some of their efforts were scarcely to be indexed as "songs." I don't think I've ever heard a real good singing voice on night watch. But I will say that the regular lyrics and the improvisations that floated through those night airs certainly belonged to our Western Americana. Most of the offerings were ballads, sentimental or sad, with a goodly sprinkle of smutty stuff, which, like all such things, contained plain, unadulterated rot along with others that were really amusing.

Those nightly songbirds were not out there vocalizing for their own appreciation, they were actually singing to soothe and reassure those spooky, cud-chewing hellions that everything was cozy and safe, and that they must all go sleepy-bye, for little Willie was out there to see that no scarey boogeyman sneaked up and kicked them in the slats. It is really a phenomenon, the reassuring influence a singing, mounted man has over a great herd of half-wild, spooky cattle.

At midnight, or thereabout, the great herd with one accord slowly rose to its feet with a sort of sigh, stretched, some took a step or two, and all soon returned to the prone position, maybe on the opposite side. The next move came with the break of day, when they once more regained their feet and commenced their grazing and drifting in the direction chosen by the herders.

All this, of course, if things went well throughout the night, and, sad to relate, things did not always go so well. A coyote's yelp, a clap of thunder, a human sneeze, a pony's neigh, the moon rising from back of the rugged mesa, anything, no matter how trivial, might touch off that great assembly as if it had been a keg of gunpowder. Then the stampede, that most dreaded of all trail possibilities!

Away they'd go in a mad, blind frenzy! A poor cowboy or two, insignificant mites on insignificant ponies, racing ahead of that uncontrollable tidal wave of wild-eyed, stark-mad longhorns. They saw nothing, they heeded nothing, they stopped at nothing. Those waddies dashing ahead in front of them could only hope, by the flashes of their six-guns or any other expedient, to gradually turn them and set them into a "mill," where, in time, they would race themselves to exhaustion going round and round and round and getting nowhere. All this at full speed generally over treacherous ground, in the black of the night, and possibly in a thunderstorm. Personally, I've never been in a night stampede, but I have helped to turn some in the daytime, and I know what it must have been. They were just one of those things that read so exciting and romantic and thrilling on the printed page, but which you wish to hell had never been invented when you're actually going through the experience. What a mess daylight disclosed! Counting noses among the boys and wondering if the absentees were still cussing in this sad vale of woes and tears, even if not in the immediate vicinity, or whether they were already riding range in that promised land they sang about in their night songs. Casualties did happen and often, too. Then the check-up on the stock at hand, and the tracking and hunting for the scattered remnants. What a mess!

150

Singing to 'em

JO MORA

Crossing a big herd over a river in freshet was the next hazard to a night stampede. Well, one thing was certain on the long trails: though there was plenty of monotonous, dull work to be done, yet when the fireworks really did commence, they were certainly varied, exciting, and dangerous. A cowboy earned his money, and at the end, when the herd had been delivered and all he had to do was to get washed up before he wandered back to Texas, believe me he was entitled to a skylark, even if only in the lurid reception centers of the cowtown terminals. And if his idea of fun so often wound up with whiskey, gunpowder, and manslaughter, it was only because his environment was in that wild frontier where so much of the society mushrooming there was loaded down with all the vices and debauchery of civilization.

A herd might be a mixed one; or of breeding stock for the upper ranges; or of beeves only. In the parlance of the range, a "beef" was a steer over four years of age. He could be twenty, for all of that, a scrawny old mossyhorn that would have to lope out twice into the sunshine to cast a shadow. But just so long as he was over four, he was a "beef"; and that was one of the difficulties the drovers had when they contracted for a herd of beeves from those easygoing Southerners. Many of the drovers did not drive their own brand, but contracted for them in the various localities of the cattle country where maybe several of the local ranchers got up a crowd to gather and put up a herd of the size and kind agreed upon. They cut out all the beeves, if that's what the contract called for, and when that drover took that herd over, I reckon he got many a jolt when he saw the passing parade at counting time. Ordinarily, a drover doing business at that game had to be a keen judge of cows, but he positively could not get hard and choosy, for he was fearful that if he did, word of his "tightness" would get abroad and then he knew he'd have to whistle the next time he wanted a herd sifted out of that brasada. So they were forced to take what was given them, and they sure enough got plenty of seedy stock along with the

1867-1880 Southwest Texas. A cow-crowd...brush poppers of the Brasada

Jo Mora

prime ones in the bargain. So, a beef was a beef if over four years of age, and many a crowbait mossyhorn made the trip north when he should have been left behind, fit only for the glue works or the tannery. However, as cattle were then also sold by the same standards at the end of the trails, and not by weight and quality, I guess it all balanced up more or less in a slip-shod manner.

The average spread of horns in a big trail herd would average about four and a half feet, with many specimens going five feet and over, and here and there record heads reaching eight feet or more. We used to hear all kinds of tall stories about these record spreads from those "who had actually seen them and would swear on oath, etc., etc.," and also from those who had not seen them "but would vouch on a stack of Bibles for the truthfulness of the informant, etc., etc."

I've heard some of these yarns that climbed to fourteen feet and better. Of course they could never lead you to any of these world wonders, but they'd swear to it with a straight face that it was God's truth nevertheless.

Right after the Spanish-American War, I saw at a fair in San Antonio, Texas, two live longhorns on exhibition that had about as fine horns as anyone would care to see. I regret now that I didn't measure their spreads, but, as I recall them after these many years, I think one of them crowded nine feet in width.

The longest I have ever actually handled and measured was seven feet ten and one half inches. I found this skull in fair shape in the heavy brush of Zapata County, and after measuring it with a knot on a stake rope, I left it there.

Later on, in San Antonio, I was with a crowd "talking longhorns," and when I mentioned this pair I was promptly offered twenty-five dollars for them, if I could produce them. This pittance was big money in those days . . . almost a cowboy's monthly wages. I was about to go by train to New Mexico, at the time, but decided to stay over. A clerk at the Menger House staked me to a good pony and a little spending money, and I headed south the next day.

It was a couple of hundred miles, more or less, to my destination, and when I got there I lost about a week hunting for those pesky horns in vain. Then I met up with an old "paisano del campo" I had ridden with on my former stay there, and he took me to them in a jiffy. He had seen them there, himself. They were a terrible nuisance to pack, but I finally worried them to the railroad and shipped them to San Antonio. Eventually I got my remaining interest in the deal, and those horns adorned the private office of a San Francisco firm, till the great fire of 1906 sent them up in smoke.

Imagine the headaches those old-time shippers must have had trying to squeeze a seven foot spread of spooky longhorns through a five-foot freight-car door. What was the answer? Well, that was a problem in lower mathematics that often took a saw to solve. A car-load of longhorns was no joke.

V

The *evolution* of the Chuck Wagon goes in two or three jumps, from the simple provisions for a few days only, tucked inside the bedroll around the remuda bell mare; to the pack mule with saddle and alforcas; to the ox-drawn cart; to the present-day chuck wagon, horse drawn and in slightly varying styles.

The very first cow-hunting crowds were generally an aggregation of ranchers, gathered to cooperate in putting up a herd to go up the trail. It is true they made up an outfit to work together in harmony, and even chose a boss from among their number to direct the operations: yet they were all independent ranchers working together for the task on hand. Maybe some of them brought along their sons, or the more prosperous, if before the Civil War, brought a Negro slave; later they had a Mexican vaquero hired hand or a black one. Each one brought along his own provisions, and menus were simple on those frontiers: bacon or sowbelly (razorbacks ran practically wild), corn meal in bulk or already baked into compact frontier bread, coffee, salt, and possibly some sugar. These were the mainstays of grub makings. Beef they killed on the range. There was nothing fancy, let me assure you, but that type of fuel would stick to your ribs, and the boys did mighty hard riding on it. Each one did his own cooking, though sometimes the grub was pooled and one or two might do the cooking for the crowd en masse.

The next step was when cows commenced to come into their own and the cattle industry really commenced to be some business. Then the crowds organized a little more and outfits were formed. These generally had a pack mule for the grub, with a regular pack saddle and alforjas (saddle boxes on the sides, of wood or rawhide) and a cook. Now these simple outfits were very good and filled all requirements where the cow work went on more or less near "home," and replenishments could be had without too much effort or loss of time. However, when it came to taking a big herd up the long trail with an outfit of hired riders that had to be fed, and traveling for weeks at a time through unpopulated country, there was no alternative but to provide some kind of a conveyance to carry sufficient provisions for these long stretches: a water barrel, the bedrolls, and the odds and ends that were absolutely necessary.

As previously stated, some of the very early ones were drawn by oxen. These were slow-moving, but, as the pace of a trail herd is anything but that of a speed burner, they seemed to fill the bill at the start. It is generally accepted, in certain trail annals, that the first real chuck wagon to go up the trail was one especially built for the purpose by that gallant old frontier cattleman, Col. Charles Goodnight. The story goes that it took ten yoke of oxen to haul it over those trails in the making. That's some team, all right, and I doubt if the boys had to give it much of a lift with their ropes and ponies at the river banks.

Many years ago I heard this argument thrashed out, that is, which really was the first chuck wagon to go "up the trail." The only records I have from my own notes, are what was told me long ago by an old rawhide, "Austin Jack" Thacker. He claimed that it was in 1857 that he went up the trail with an outfit belonging to a stockman named McCutcheon, and that they had a "camp cart." He said there were not then the well-established trails of later years. He also stated that they came within an ace of losing that cart and he his life while crossing the Missouri, fifteen or twenty miles below Kansas City. However, they all got over safely and trailed across the State of Missouri and sold the herd at the Mississippi River near Hannibal.

Outfit chuck cart on the early cattle trails.

This same old cowboy, Austin Jack, also claimed to have ridden with another trail outfit that likewise had a "camp wagon." This herd belonged to a well-known rancher and drover named Reed, and they trailed through Louisiana for the New Orleans market. He said the Civil War broke out before they had delivered the herd. That sets the date at 1861. My old notes are a little confusing in this matter, but I'm quite sure he said that the later-famous "Shanghai Pierce" had been a waddie of his on that trip. He further declared that the camp wagon got to be quite a problem, at times, through the Louisiana swamps. Also that the drover, Jim Reed, joined the Confederacy, lost an arm in the cause, yet returned to Texas to be just as efficient a cowman as he had ever been, and got to be one of the best known drovers of the long trails in the later 60's and 70's. Now, if Austin Jack told the truth, and I have every reason to believe he did, I would say that the cart with the McCutcheon outfit, if not the very first, was certainly one of the first.

There was no particular style to those first old camp wagons, and they were mostly the typical ox cart of those days, made up with hoops to take a tarpaulin as a cover in rainy weather. They carried a water barrel with a good tight lid for the rough trails, and generally had a double yoke of oxen. They answered the purpose fairly well, but it was

158

soon found that they were too slow. Not that any particular speed was needed in following the plodding herd, but there were times when it was found expedient to hurry the wagon ahead, possibly to ford a river and establish a camp on the other side before the herd arrived; or for a fast drive to some nearby settlement for provisions or other necessities; or for some other of the countless emergencies that might arise.

So it was perfectly natural that the next move in the evolution was to a horse-drawn wagon, generally with a team of four, sometimes six. In a short time after its introduction, a large upright box was bolted at the tail gate. Its front cover was hinged at the bottom, and when opened would swing down till at right angles and held there by ropes, chains, or a heavy prop to the ground. This made a very fine working table for the cook. The inside of the box was divided into compartments and shelves, large or small to suit the individual taste of the owner, and primarily designed to hold the various items in the make-up of the provisions. This invention took hold fast and before long it got to be the regular style in chuck wagons. Of course, there were some without it. It goes without saying that hoops were always carried for the usual tarpaulin cover when necessary, as likewise the water barrel.

The chuck wagon was the "carry-all," the traveling storeroom, wardrobe, and closet of the outfit. Here, besides the provisions for the inner man, were the cooking utensils, the Dutch ovens, the skillets, the pots, and the pans; the table service (you might call it the knee or lap service) of tin plates and cups, with knives, forks, and spoons. There were also the fire irons and pot hooks, axes, crowbar, shovel, and when on roundup, the branding irons. Here, too, the bedrolls, and any small bits of personal plunder a rider might have that he did not roll up with his blankets. A banjo or a guitar might sometimes be found. Fancy suitcases, week-end kits, and hatboxes were not to be found there. You see, the boys did not dress for dinner; the truth is, they didn't always undress to go to bed. There was mighty little shaving done en route, and

Wolfing a bait at the

when those cowboys jammed the breeze into town at the trail's end, they were a push-over for the frontier barbers.

Wagon cooks ran the full gamut of culinary endeavor or ability, from marvelous efficiency to criminal uselessness. Plenty in the latter category, too. Cooking over a campfire, especially for a considerable number of men, is an art. Nothing short of it. I've cooked for myself alone for many years over a campfire, so I think I know what I'm talking about in that respect. I'm not boasting of my abilities, I'm just stating that I am qualified to judge. To the dude on an outdoor vacation, the exhilaration of the open spaces and the very novelty of it can shed a cloak of romance over a lot of very punk cooking; but to the man who is living and working on it, day in day out, there's mighty little romance to it unless it *is* good. Of course, the old-time cooks on the trails had the advantage that if you didn't like it you could leave it; and if you left it you just didn't eat, unless you killed the cook and assumed

160

chuck wagon.

JO MORA

the responsibility yourself, for the boys had to eat. They might back
you up in your act of justifiable manslaughter, but they'd never let you
off from taking up where the other let go.

There was no one particular type for trail cooks, except possibly
that there were very few young men at it. They were generally middle-
aged or older men, and he might be a native or a "furriner." He might
be a Negro, or a "Portugee," or a Mexican, or a runaway sailor. He
might be one that took his work with interest and did give the boys the
best that he could conjure from the materials he was given to juggle,
and was proud of his efforts. Yet he might also be one of those un-
imaginative robots with a crude routine of frying his greasy meat and
potatoes, turning out rubber biscuits or crude corn bread, and brewing
a slop he called coffee. Yet why discourse? It's just the same as in
ordinary city life, nothing more, nothing less; except that cooking over
a campfire with the wind blowing ashes, sand, dirt and whatnot into

161

the laboratory added a handicap not easy to overcome by the careless slob.

However, to hark back over the years, I can recall many a fine meal concocted by chuck wagon cooks. Real fine examples of what can be done by good operators over a campfire with Dutch oven, skillet, and pot. So, let's forget the bad ones, and smack our lips on the thoughts of those that were good. Cowboys had their own names for many a range titbit, some of them of Spanish influence, others in plain, bald United States.

I'll never forget one such cowboy dinner, though it wasn't from a chuck wagon. This was back in 1906, in the White Mountains of Arizona Territory. I was on a grizzly hunt with a grand pal, the late Lorenzo Hubbell, Indian trader of Tusayan. Our little outfit consisted of a wagon which Hubbell drove, with a fine span at the pole, Monte and Star, that were also top saddle horses. We had with us a Navajo as a swamper and horse wrangler. He and I were in the saddle. We also had with us a Mexican sheep herder that Hubbell knew and had picked up at St. Johns. He was to take us to a spot where he had seen grizzlies that Spring.

We were first going to hunt in the Forest Reserve and had emerged from the woods and dropped into a fine potrero that stretched before us like a great bowl in the mountains. The floor was as flat as a table. A little log cabin was in view, with a thin column of smoke rising from its chimney. A white pony was standing saddled in front, several others grazed in the distance. Hubbell called out to me as he pointed towards the cabin.

"I guess old man Slaughter is gathering his mountain stock for the Winter. We'll camp right here."

So we all reined up and commenced making camp. I had already made a second trip to the vicinity of the wagon, dragging in dry firewood with my rope and pony, when we noticed a figure come out of

162

the cabin, ease into the saddle, and lope leisurely over to us. He knew Hubbell and greetings were exchanged. I was then introduced. This cowboy was old man Slaughter's son. After the first exchange of small talk he said, "Just thought you'd like to drift over to the cabin. We're having a son-of-a-bitch for supper. Better come over pronto, plenty for everybody."

"Thanks" Hubbell answered with that boyish, dancing-eyed smile he had. "We'll be right over."

Slaughter wheeled his pony and loped back. This was a new one to me, but, not wishing to show my ignorance, I never batted an eyelash and just waited for Hubbell to further elucidate on this invite to such a cannibalistic prospect. But he remained quite unruffled and non-communicative, just hurrying at his chores.

We all soon started walking over to the cabin, and I must admit that curiosity got the better of me, and I asked, "What in hell is a son-of-a-bitch? I've known lots of them but I never thought I'd ever be asked to eat one."

Hubbell laughed. "Oh, that? Thought you knew. It's a marrow gut stew."

We were already at the door and, as we entered, the odor emanating from that pot on the stove was the unadulterated ambrosia of the gods to us. The elder Slaughter was there and another cowboy, a taller, well-appearing young man. The latter had been doing the cooking. After a short conversational résumé on cows, pasture, weather and hunting, we all sat down, set our bellies to the board, and the unmentionable was passed around in two pans. Then the cook swung open the oven door and produced a couple of pans of biscuits, as golden topped, light and tasty as I've ever had. I may have had as good since, but certainly never any better. And, Emily Post notwithstanding, we mopped up that exceptionally fine stew with our biscuits to the last smitch. Of course we had the usual black coffee of every cow camp,

163

and for dessert—you bet we had dessert—hot, dried-apple pie. And was it good! And there was one cowboy dinner, just stew, biscuits, coffee and pie, that I'll never forget to the day old Gabe takes down his saxophone and gives me the toot to report for roll call. You might say some of it was due to the snappy title of the entrée; but, be that as it may, it was good, lickin' good.

Now, there's another cowboy meal that also stands out in my memory with positive red letters. It was of such an exotic, "uncowboy" complexion, although strictly a chuck-wagon affair, that it rates as one of those never to be forgotten. I was not riding for anybody, at the time, but had just completed one of those grand skylarks of youth, and was taking a long pasear in the saddle, making a wide, wide circle that would finally land me back to my stamping ground in northern Arizona. I had been with a bunch of Navajos (I was the only white man in the bunch) and we had ridden north to race ponies with the Utes of southern Colorado and Utah. This had been one of the very few times I had ever been lucky gambling with poor, innocent, unsophisticated Lo. Though the many years passed since then have fogged my memory a bit as to minute details, I can recall a gorgeous silver-and-turquoise concha belt, a double handful of silver buttons, and an exceptionally fine Navvy pony (and there were some good ones) which I was then riding. My "old reliable" I had relegated to the job of packing my bedroll and simple camp outfit. This was in the San Juan country of southern Colorado, and I was jogging along leisurely, when a rider overtook me.

He was a pleasant, middle-aged stockman riding a good-looking horse. We engaged in the usual small talk of the range and I got a kick out of watching him trying to size me up. I had on a well-worn pair of silver-mounted California spurs, my bit was a straight shank Las Cruces with silver concha, yet my saddle was an old double cinch of Denver make. My two ponies were unbranded. But he asked no personal questions. So, in the course of our conversation, I gradually told him what his curiosity wanted to know. He also enlightened me with the fact that he was foreman of a wagon outfit camped some miles ahead and which we should reach about supper time. They were waiting for a small herd, I think it was just a couple hundred head of graded heifers and cows, and some thoroughbred bulls. This was breeding stock they were to drive to their home ranch—I can't remember the brand—in southeastern Colorado or northern New Mexico. But that's neither here nor there as far as this incident is concerned. He had ridden, the day before, to some station on the Denver and Rio Grande where he had been in telegraphic communication with the home ranch for certain orders. He was an agreeable companion and time passed easily as the miles slipped by. He had visited once in San Francisco at the time of the Midwinter Fair, and he thought the city by the Golden Gate was the finest town he had ever seen. He invited me to camp with the outfit till the herd arrived, and offered me a job on the drive if I wanted it. Said he had the finest wagon cook in the Southwest, barring none: a "furriner" from Spain. Thought he was a Basque. Only had three cowboys with him, but all were top hands. And so passed the afternoon, till the sun, at our backs, commenced losing altitude and lengthened our shadows grotesquely ahead of us. Then we rounded a mesa point and popped into the wagon camp.

Supper was ready and waiting for us. I unsaddled and unpacked, turned my ponies loose with their cavvy, and squatted down in the circle to see what could be done about the rumblings of the inner man. It was a good, simple meal, with just that little something about it that made you realize it was no ordinary hand that had cooked it. I can't remember what the meat was, but I think it was a stew of some sort. I do remember distinctly, however, some excellent corn bread, that fluffy delicate type you seldom find in cow camps, and for dessert a kind of Brown Betty of dried apples and a sauce that was distinctive.

Not that what we had had was the greatest meal ever, but I could realize that the cook who produced it might easily justify the wagon boss' boast to me that he was the "best damned wagon cook in the Southwest" if given the ingredients and the incentive.

The cook himself was a short, powerfully built man, reddish hair heavily sprinkled with gray, silent and rather grouchy looking. After the meal, we got up and put our tin plates, which had been well mopped up with that last piece of corn bread, together with the cups and other implements into the "wreck tub" under the chuck-box table. I could speak Spanish fluently, yet I said nothing to him in his native tongue, though I did tell him in English that he had served a mighty good meal. This he accepted with the momentary flash of a grateful smile, and slightly nodded his head in acknowledgment of my compliment.

It was one of those gorgeous evenings when a big happy moon rises in the East long before the sun calls it a day. You might say we blended in one continuous wave from the warm glow of a fine sunset to the cold blue of a full moon without any apparent transition. We had had a satisfying meal, we were at peace with the world, and there was little to worry about as we propped our backs on our bedrolls and saddles. We swapped yarns as we smoked. The cook busied himself with a wad of dough, and after considerable kneading and patting, he placed the mass in a pan, covered it with a flour-sack towel, and placed it down on the ground a short distance from the campfire. Then he busied himself somewhere out of range of our vision.

Suddenly we heard the crash of tin pans and rattling utensils as a horse popped into view from the shadow of the chuckbox, a quarter-filled flour sack in his teeth. He gave this a couple of violent shakes, scattering a generous nebula of flour all over the immediate scene. In unison we all gave a shout, when suddenly from out of nowhere that cook landed into the center of the picture with the most gorgeous burst of profanity in a foreign tongue! It was delivered with that vehemence and timing that proved beyond all doubt it was no amateur at the source. And that horse dropped the sack like it had burned his lips and clattered off. He was one of the chuck-wagon wheelers, and one of those camp pets and pests that are always walking over everything and nibbling at anything from potato peelings to cold biscuits. An equine nuisance if ever there was one.

When that verbal masterpiece and our laughter subsided sufficiently, I turned to the foreman, next to me, and whispered, "Hell, that hombre's no Basque."

"Do you savvy his noise?" I was asked.

"Sure I do," I answered. "There's only one race on earth can cuss as well as that. This bird's a Catalan."

"Let's hear you talk to him. Tell 'im we agree with everything he's said."

I thought for a moment, then called out to him in his own native Catalan tongue, prefacing my remarks with as tart an opener as I could command, then stated I was proud to hear a man in that cow camp who really knew how to express himself.

He wheeled around in unmistakable surprise, and, still holding the flour sack he had retrieved, he came over and squatted down in front of me. He rattled off in the language of his heart with an eagerness that betrayed a lonesome soul expanding. In answer to his first question, I explained that I was the son of a Catalonian, and that broke his reserve completely and he told me the story of his life, in the terse, almost brusque manner of his kind. His name was Carléts (little Carlos) yet they called him Carl, at the ranch, which, along with his red hair, made people think he was a German. He shrugged his shoulders at this and tilted his head with a "What can you do about it?" grimace. He had been a ship's cook on a "Spain to South America" east coast run. Then he had changed to another Spanish line, New York to Barcelona. After

167

a few trips he took French leave and stayed in New York without a passport. They were not very particular in those days. Worked his way south down the east coast, and finally wound up cooking at one of the well-known restaurants in New Orleans. But the wanderlust had him and he shipped on a sailing schooner to Corpus Christi, Texas. There he got a job as wagon cook on a big cow outfit—from Goliad County, I think it was. He was with them a couple of years, then had a serious run-in with a drunken cattle buyer. He had to quit on a fast horse, though helped in every way by his outfit. He gave no further details, so I'm sure I didn't ask for any. Next he was cooking, or as he stated it, trying to cook, at a gold mine in the high Rockies of Colorado; but he didn't stay long. Said it wasn't worth the trouble trying to be a cook where boiling water wouldn't produce a soft-boiled egg. That's the way he put it and his accompanying gestures were a laugh. So he drifted below and wound up as a cow-ranch cook once more with this outfit. Said they treated him very fine both at the ranch and when with the wagon. However, he felt he might be drifting south into Mexico next year, to the capital maybe, where there were many of his countrymen. He was just plain lonesome for his kind.

At this point he abruptly stopped his narrative to lapse into wrinkled-brow thought for a moment. Then he turned to the wagon boss and said in English, "Luke 'ere, Don Jeem, how many more day we stay 'ere, new cows doan come?"

"Well, I'd say two days more, maybe three before the herd gets here."

"Mañana, no? For sure, eh?" And when assured that the expected herd could not arrive on the morrow for certain, he said with an air of finality, "Aw rite. Now I tell it to you. Mañana I cook, and thees not cowboy grub. Thees for caballeros. No? Thees my deena, Carléts' treat. Thees joven"—and he pointed to me—"muy simpatico, no? I cook for him."

He stood up abruptly without a word, walked over to the chuck box, dusted the mauled flour sack and put it away. He never spoke another word, but we could hear him winding his alarm clock and making up his bed on the opposite side of the wagon.

The next day we all gave a grand imitation, as Jim, the wagon boss, put it, of "the idle rich busy doing nothing." I should not have said "all," because Carléts was busier'n a bird dog in a quail cover all day long. We had a swim in the river, and when I went back to the wagon to get something from my bedroll, Carléts was there alone, and he winked at me and motioned me up into the wagon where he was. He showed me a wooden chest, with a padlocked lid, which he kept under the wagon seat. Inside, apart from some personal plunder, were two packing cases with his name and address on Express stickers from a well-known Spanish importing house in New York. With dancing eyes he pried open the tops and exposed a veritable gourmet's delight in Spanish goodies. There were cans of imported olive oil, fish, various chorizos, sobrasada, butifarras, and longanizas (the latter ones choice types of pork sausages). There were half a dozen dried, salted codfish, garvanzos, chocolates, some little boxes of Cuban pasta de guayava, Spanish pastas (somewhat like noodles) and a dozen or more quart bottles of red wine with their straw covers. I've mentioned only a part of what was there, for, though time dulls my memory, I never really did know all that was there. Suffice it to say that it was an assortment chosen by a top cook who certainly knew his Spanish onions.

He told me that he never used any of these ingredients on the trail or round-up camp, and that they were his own private property. However, he informed me that he had been treated so well by the big boss, the owner of the ranch, who was some sort of a politician or a bigwig at Washington, that he (Carléts) had made up his mind to give him a Catalonian dinner he'd not soon forget, when next he visited the ranch with his family, as he often did. He laughingly said he had packed those precious ingredients along with him wherever he went, as he would not trust them with the Mexican number two cook left in charge at the ranch cookhouse.

But I must make a long story short. That evening we squatted down to positively the most out-of-the-ordinary and tastiest dinner a crowd of cowboys ever had at their chuck wagon. Here's how the menu stacked up: We started out with cold, shredded codfish flakes, olives from Spain, sliced raw onions, and all with a dressing of imported olive oil and wine vinegar. Then some slices of langoniza (something like salami) with a dash of garlic and some herbs. Then, served in our tin coffee cups, we had a heavy soup, a sort of purée with—now get a load of this—fried crispy croutons. After that he passed around in tin plates a very curious-looking concoction that had them guessing but which I immediately recognized: calamares con tinta (squid in their ink). As most know, a squid is a little cuttlefish which, when pursued, ejects an inky fluid to cover his retreat. These imported squids (in cans) were cooked in rice with their "ink," and the ensemble took on a very dark gray tone. It is a most delicious bit when properly cooked, and this one certainly was, yet it is one of those "foreign morsels" that you are either crazy about or crazy if you eat it. The boys all liked it, yet when they were told just what it was and how come, a couple ruffled their noses and commenced telling about other funny things they had eaten and still lived to tell the tale.

Then came a real Catalan Olla Podrida, the peer of which would be hard to find; though poor Carléts, with his artist's pride, almost cried as he lamented the absence in it of a chicken and a couple of minor ingredients. Olla means pot, and podrida means rotten . . . rotten pot; surely not a very appetizing name in English, but it's a famous Spanish dish, and every province makes it in its own way. It has everything in it from the piano stool to the kitchen lamp, yet in the hands of a real cook is something very fine. This one had beef, a ham bone, salt pork, several different chorizos, pastas, spuds, carrots and onions. Like most Spanish dishes, it was touched up a bit with saffron, but not too much. However, let me tell you it was delicious, for this homely mélange, made by an artist, can be a masterpiece. And this one was all of that!

I forgot to state that when he brought on the squids he also uncorked a couple of bottles of that red wine, and asked me, in Catalan, to explain to the rest in better English than he could command, that with a meal of this type the Lord would be very angry if anyone ate it without wine. He added a cute simile, saying these were "agullas d'enfilá vi." Needles to be threaded with wine.

And so we wined and dined, and were just about as full as ticks, when he served us with a sort of crepe or light pancake, rolled and sprinkled with sugar, with Cuban guayava inside. Black coffee.

Boy! There was a dinner! If any of the other participants of that night's festivities are still alive, I'll bet they agree with me that there was the grandest and most out-of-the-ordinary chuck-wagon meal cowboys ever had. My main worry, after that, was how I could show my appreciation, for, after all, he had given us that feast in my honor, with wine and imported goods that were his own private property. I knew his independent, brusque type, too. His kind can't be tipped. But that's another yarn and we must get back to wagon outfits once more.

By no means is the chuck wagon an adjunct of the great herds on the long trails only; they are also just as much a part of the round-ups, past and present. By the way, round-ups are also called rodéos in California and adjacent ranges, and Mexico. Notice the way the word is accented. Nowadays, in parts away from California, the word is pronounced ródeo, and is applied generally to the cowboy shows now so prevalent all over the West and many parts of the East also.

The round-up originated in the more northern and western parts of Texas where cowboys could work and control large herds of cattle under organized leadership with a freedom that was positively out of the question in the dense mesquitales of the South. In the late 70's, a system of round-ups by districts was adopted in Texas on a real organized basis.

In the days of the open range, cows of many brands naturally intermingled and formed a pattern like a well-shuffled deck, and many owners contributed their cowboys to the great round-ups. Large herds were gathered on those fenceless ranges, and at some chosen spot well adapted for the work to be done, the cutting out and the branding took place. Steers were separated from cows and calves, and the work of branding the calf crop and the mavericks commenced.

Naturally, a calf belonged to the brand of the mother. In the matter of slick-ears and mavericks (unbranded stock) their branding and distribution was not such an easy matter. In Texas, before the Civil War, when cattle were cheap, plentiful, and with few markets, there was no particular set law concerning slick-ears that had been weaned and were not following the mother. But later on, when cows became valuable, the laws, written and unwritten, about the branding of slick-ears were accepted and carried out by a very few "honest" cattlemen at their face value; though many of the interpretations of these laws were carried out according to who was or was not looking, and the momentary elasticity of the conscience. Whenever a rider came upon a maverick, if he could catch it, throw it, and hog-tie it, he'd slap his brand on it p.d.q. There were also agreements and what-nots about outsiders branding calves that were with their mothers, applying the legal brand, and getting so much per head from the rightful owner.

At the round-ups, of course, the maverick problem was different. There they were cut out and disposed of according to whatever agreement had been made by the various owners concerned, or according to what might be the accepted custom of the locality. They might be parceled out then and there to the various brands represented, in proportion to the number of cows each had there. Or they might be pooled

172

and auctioned off and the proceeds divided in proportion. Or in any similar manner.

A whole chapter, in fact a volume, could be written about the history of branding calves and mavericks, the various interpretations and the abuses of the laws controlling same. Some of it is not such pretty history, but it is sure enough full of knavery, gunfire, violence, and death. Such a lengthy discussion here would be quite beyond the objective of this volume. Considerable has been written on this question already, and some of it contains excellent historical data for those really interested in the evolution of the cattle industry in these United States.

I have heard two or three varying stories on the origin of the word "Maverick" as applied to a slick-ear or unbranded "cow." I guess the one most accepted is as follows: There was a Colonel Samuel A. Maverick, a Texan from San Antonio, who, about the middle of the last century, received five hundred longhorns as payment of a debt in lieu of cash. Not being a stockman, he turned the herd out on a ranch some distance away, in the custody of a Negro slave family. The latter, not being closely watched, became very lax in attending to the herd, especially in the matter of branding the calves. After a few years, there were hundreds

173

of slick-ears on that range, and when this condition became particularly noticeable, many enterprising neighbors commenced to do a little branding on their own hook and with their own irons. It got to be quite the stunt in that locality, and the saying got to be, "Let's go brand some Mavericks." There were no telephones or telegraphs or even efficient mail service there in those days, yet the news traveled by that inexplicable "underground" of the old range, and this expression spread fast and far. A word had been coined, and "maverick" has been the accepted term for the unbranded "cow" in all corners of cattleland from that day to this.

Round-ups were held in the Spring and Fall. The former was the more important and the busier one, for here it was that the calf crop was branded. The Fall one might be for the purpose of cutting out the beeves that were prime for the late market and those selected for special winter feeding.

Anyhow, it was the great "social event" of Cowboydom. Here it was that old cronies met after a year, or years, of not having seen each other; and the preparations, as "the clans gathered" before the event, were busy ones indeed, yet full of fun and interest. Riggings were overhauled and put in top shape; broncs were topped by the professional busters; cowboys worked out their rough strings; and at night around the campfire was animated and friendly camaraderie. There were stories aplenty, with a small percentage funny and many more supposed to be. Anyhow, most of them were of the smutty brand and not particularly well told. There were songs, lots of them. Some prime candidates for the files of our Americana; others, if not so prime, at least runners-up and amusing. I can't recall having ever heard a real fine voice around these campfires. Sometimes the boys brought along a musical instrument and I can recall having heard at various times guitars, fiddles, jew's-harps, harmonicas, accordions and banjos. The same applies to the instruments as to the voices: I never heard a real talented musician or one that had the earmarks of a "comer" in these round-up circles, though much of the stuff heard was mighty pleasing and amusing.

"Reps," with their remudas, drifted in, and old acquaintances were renewed and new ones made. A Rep, or "stray man," is a representative of a ranch whose cattle were likely to have strayed into the range to be worked over. As such he was there to look out for the interests of the brand he represented; to brand the calves belonging to his iron; getting his share of slick-ears; and cutting out and driving his stock back to the home range.

Then, on the appointed day, the chuck wagon drove out to the camp appointed for the first circle, followed by the wranglers herding the remuda. The cowboys gathered there later.

In the wee small hours of the next morning, to the shouted "get up" orders of the cook in his own version of how a cowboy's breakfast should be announced, the waddies rolled out from under their bed tarps, squeezed into their boots, and proceeded to bolt a bait and wash it down with black coffee stout enough to float a bolt washer. The night-hawk brought in the remuda, and it was quickly encircled by the temporary rope corral, into which the boys shuffled quietly, dragging their loops. The day's pony was soon caught, saddles were adjusted, and before long the superintendent of the round-up gave his orders, told of the various sections of that range to be worked over, and parceled off the little groups of circle riders. Then they started easing into the saddles. There might be an argument or two with touchy ponies that couldn't seem to get the kinks out of their spines till they warmed up. But it wasn't long before they all started riding out of camp. Little by little, pairs or small groups of riders dropped out and turned off to one side or another to cover the various sections they had been chosen to work over. The great circle drag was on.

Flats, chaparrals, mesa tops, canyons, barrancas, creek beds and river bottoms all are thoroughly combed and any hiding cows kicked out. Cattle ahead seem to sense what's coming and start moving at all gaits. A big, fat bull lowing soft and deep at every step shuffles along quietly; cows trot along short distances with their attending calves, and then turn abruptly to size up the situation, all eyes and ears; steers and long yearlings may come boiling up over the canyon rim and dash ahead like scared deer. Some may try to double back, and the boys then have to ride and ride hard sometimes, too. But the bunches ahead keep getting bigger and bigger, and all gravitate in one direction. Then other groups drift in from the sides, and, eventually, the combined big, bawling, restless herd fusses around in a great cloud of dust on the chosen round-up ground.

Not far from there the chuck wagon has already moved in, hours before, and the cook has dinner ready. The herd is held by a few of the boys, according to its size and spookiness, and the rest race into camp with a whoop and a holler. Dusty, sweat-caked ponies are unsaddled and turned loose, and with noses to the ground and gradually bending knees they circle around and it's but a few seconds before they are taking that roll and back scratch that means so much to them. Then a good shake and they wander slowly away, seemingly well aware that their duty for the day has been fulfilled, and you may drag or twirl a rope near them without any undue alarm or suspicion on their part. But what a different story the next morning!

If the circle had not been too large and the riders brought in their herd by noon or thereabout, they'd do the parting and branding that same afternoon. Otherwise it would be done the next day. And that's when the cowboys would catch up their best cutting ponies. It was then that the waddies, who forked those top ponies that could cut didos on a two-bit piece, had it all over the ones who had to try to rein a stiff-necked jughead. What a difference in ponies! And, by the same token, what a difference in cowboys, too!

The Rep

JO MORA

A real cowboy, on a real horse, could sift into that herd like they were both asleep, and yet the cow that had been picked for the cutting soon found itself on the outside edge of the herd without suspecting there was any dirty work contemplated, and heading out into the open spaces before it realized what it was all about. If it tried to dive back, that pesky pony and rider were right there in the way; if it darted this way, so did they; if it plunged that way, there they were. Then a sudden wave of an arm, an explosive yelp, the sharp crack of quirt on chap leather, the unexpected lunge of the pony, and that critter would be heading out once more and going fast. A short, fast run and a quick stop for pony and rider if that cow showed the proper inclination to keep on going. If not, then of course further sharp maneuvering, twisting and turning, ever heading that stubborn one till it decided to go, and did go, where the rider intended it should.

A poor hand would mess into that herd fussing and cussing till he got the whole herd hot and bothered and his own pony properly lathered up. Then, after all, he might need a couple of waddies to help him turn and persuade a thoroughly stirred up and wild-eyed critter to go where it had, by that time, made up its stubborn mind it just wouldn't go. It took no great expert to pick the cowboys from the pumpkin rollers on the cutting grounds.

And so another herd was gradually built up some distance away, which we called the "day herd." Into this went the steers and bulls, and, in fact, everything but the cows with calves, and the mavericks to be branded. When those to be branded had been attended to, they were turned loose onto the range. Well, there was an exception, and that was the cows and calves belonging to outside brands. These, after they had been attended to, were turned into the day herd which was taken along each day or as the round-up progressed and the branding grounds changed. Naturally it kept getting bigger and bigger until the work was done, and the various Reps cut out their stock and drove it

The Cutting Pony.

JO MORA

back to their own ranges and the home stock was disposed of as the owners might plan.

Now, a word or two about the branding and the marking of cattle. If there are a dozen ways to skin a cat, there are a dozen and one ways to handle a branding party. As I sit here writing about this phase of a cowboy's chores, my mind goes wandering back over the scenes of yesteryears, and it's then I realize what a varied lot of ways there are to do the trick. Well, that's perfectly understandable, for although the ultimate objective is the same—that is, to catch that calf or full grown maverick and hold it quiet long enough to copyright it—two persons seldom do things in exactly the same way. No more than that all men buy the same kind of a hat and wear it in the same way, though the desired objective of covering the dome is just the same.

In the cattle business, apart from dairy and fancy show stock, "cows" are raised to eventually turn into beef; and as steer meat is the tenderest and best for human consumption, bull calves are castrated and, with some outfits, heifer calves are spayed. However, in the years long past when I rode range, I never happened to work with an outfit at branding time that spayed their heifers. We just cut the bulls and let the heifers go for cow-beef or for breeders. In later years nearly all the outfits I knew vaccinated.

Branding is done with a hot iron which burns through the hair and scorches the hide so that a permanent scar is left over which the hair will not grow again. Besides this, most outfits also slit the ears with some registered distinguishing mark, and many also dewlap. To dewlap is to cut or slit the dewlap so that when healed it will hang in a certain distinguishable way. Brands have to be registered to be of any value, and a description of one might read as follows: "John Henry Jones, Postoffice Address—Apache Crossing, Coconino County, Arizona Territory. Brand—Circle M on left hip. Ear Marks—Under and over bit on

180

left and swallow fork on right. Single dewlap. Range—Black Mesa and vicinity, Coconino County, A.T."

The little, old, one-horse newspapers of Cattleland always ran ranch owners' ads. They were small affairs, generally one column across, with those priceless old-time cuts of cattle and horses to visually support the written description of the brand. Often they offered rewards for the return of strays; or they expressed their views, mostly very generous, on needy settlers openly beefing and skinning one of their cows; or plainly stating what blotters or tamperers of that brand might expect if caught. Many of these were most amusing, and gave the owners and editors wonderful opportunities to air their humor in the high falutin phrases of the period, often the better to emphasize their violent censure. To me those ads will always be priceless highlights in our Western Americana.

There are two different types of branding irons: the stamp iron and the running iron. Although there is no specification as to what material the branding iron must be made of, the very name of it denotes what most of them are. I have seen them made from any old castoff scrap just so long as the blacksmith could be wheedled into accepting it as "possible makings." I have also seen a couple made of copper, and have heard of several made of aluminum. I've also seen a few made pretty fancy with twisted shanks and fancy wrought handles. But these examples that look more like a rococo fireplace poker than a cowman's iron are not to be considered in character for Cattleland. The typical iron will average two or three feet in length, sometimes better, and about three-quarter inch in thickness, with the handle end made into a loop or ring of some kind to better control the action of the thrust when branding, and also used for hanging up on a nail or peg when not in use. Sometimes they are made with a wooden handle which is like a tube eight or ten inches long with a hole drilled into it lengthwise part of the way to take the end of shank. The truth is that irons get mighty hot during a day's work, and heat has a pesky way of crawling up that shank and into the handle which is supposed to be kept cool enough for a waddie to manipulate without having to cuss. Most of us wore gloves in the old days, and believe me they were not what a Frenchy would call "de trop" at a branding spree. However, I have been caught without gloves and have operated with a gunnysack and a bandana. I've seen a cowboy use his vest to be able to better juggle a too short handled iron. Just remember this: they do get hot!

Fires for the branding are made from any fuel that's handy, but on certain ranges firewood is as scarce at the branding grounds as the proverbial hen's teeth. Then they use chips, and these, when right, make a good, concentrated fire. In lieu of these, the chuck wagon may pack in the necessary firewood from many miles away. In later years I have seen outfits that used a sheet-iron stove. Just a simple, large cylinder open at the top. It holds the irons well and conserves fuel.

The die, or stamp, for the brand design, is made of a flat iron; maybe from a piece of regular strap iron, or a wagon tire, or any old thing hammered into shape averaging about one-quarter inch, more or less according to size and the sharp angles in the design. Of course, no matter how rough the workmanship may be, like any proper stamp the face of it should be on a flat plane. Although nothing out of the ordinary, there still is quite a trick in properly applying the stamp. Irons are not used when red hot, though this seems to be the general idea with outsiders. The important thing is to know when the iron is right. This just takes experience, for an iron that's too hot will roast the flesh unmercifully, blot the brand (specially if it's a tricky one) and is liable to leave a wound that may get infected. Then again, if it's too cold, it is liable to just leave a sore spot and not a brand. It should be hot enough to burn the hair at once and just quickly sear the surface of the hide and not through to the flesh. This then forms a quick scab, peels off nicely in

Running iron

Branding irons

Brands

IRONS

Brands

A steeple fork A bit An undersharp An underslope

A split A crop

A swallow fork An overslope

EAR MARKS A dewlap dewlaps EAR MARKS

Branding a big maverick.

Team roping "rasslin' a calf." A well attended calf.

Jo Mora

time, and leaves a permanent normal scar over which the hair will no longer grow. The stamp should be kept clean to make a sharp brand, by twirling flat on the ground, but see to it that no sand packs into the crevices with burned hair and hide.

The other type of branding iron is the "running iron." These average in length about the same as the other, but have no stamp at the recording end, set at right angle. I've seen them made in scores of different ways: some with just a slight curl at the end; some with a "fishhook"; some with a complete circle, etc., etc. All it really needs is a smooth surface (preferably round) and slightly curved that it may travel readily over the hairy hide on its scorching mission.

The stamping iron, as the name indicates, is a mechanically made die that stamps its design at one quick pressing. The running iron is nothing more or less than a big hot pencil for the "artist" to draw his design free-handed on that hide. There are no set standards for the size of a brand. It is just put there for ready reference at some distance and it's a matter of personal taste, with, of course, some consideration for the value of the hide after skinning. These stamps will run three or four or six inches or even better. Those used on horses are generally smaller than for cattle. In the early days, however, brands made with a running iron really did run and no fooling. They just about plastered the whole side of a cow. Some even branded on both sides. Why it is, no one really knows, though many theories are advanced, but the popular custom now is to brand on the left side on the hip. Bear in mind, this is no set rule; though it is the great average.

Brands made with the free-hand technique of the running iron are much easier to alter than the stamped ones, and for this reason many States legally abolished the use of the running iron. Well, the stockmen were getting desperate over the operations of the rustlers, and maybe that expedient did help a little to check the abuses of the brand blotters. However, please notice that I said "help a little." It was about as effective

184

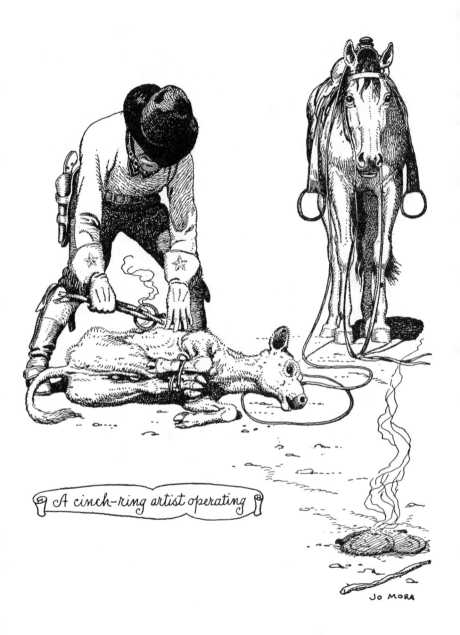

A cinch-ring artist operating

JO MORA

as the Eighteenth Amendment was in eliminating the promiscuous gargling of the merry mucilage throughout this pure land of ours. The honest cattleman ceased to pack his running iron tied to the saddle, though the crook could always pack a shorter one in his bootleg, or in the folds of his slicker. Likewise bear in mind that a pothook from the camp cooking layout or a cinch ring properly heated and held by the bent green branch of some local brush can do the trick in the hands of an expert. However, it is no easy stunt for a good job. And such was life in "the wild and woolly West." Anyhow, I think that the subject of easy brands to blot, and tough ones, and those that could not be altered, has furnished more material for cowboy conversation around the old camp-fire than any other subject. Many and many a brand has been drawn out on the smoothed-out dirt to better illustrate the conversation.

The "reading" of brands is done in a language all its own, and I could fill a tome on this topic; and a mighty interesting and amusing one it is, too, for the "fan" on range lore. However, for the purpose of this book please refer to the illustrated page on this subject which will show in a brief, general way, the nomenclature of the Western Brand.

Now let's drift back to those different ways the branding job is done. For instance, here's the old California way, with vaqueros riding center-fire saddles and taking their dallies with rawhide reatas. They didn't believe much in walking, those old paisanos, and the only bipeds at a branding would be the ones juggling the branding irons and the knife. Sometimes one man attended to both operations. Maybe an Indian tended fire, but he didn't count. There were no bull-doggers, for here they used the team roping system. A team consisted of two mounted ropers, one to lass the cow by the head, the other by the hind legs. The head roper would ease into the herd and catch his calf or slick-ear by the neck, and taking his dallies, drag it out to a spot near the fire. His partner would now ride up, and as the calf pirouetted pro-testingly at the end of the reata, he'd snap his loop around those hind

186

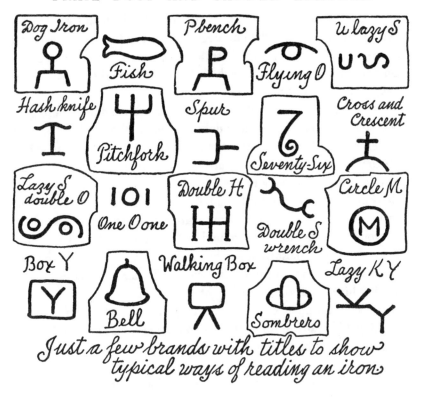

Just a few brands with titles to show typical ways of reading an iron

legs, take up his slack and dallies, and back away. It's needless to say that the patient was soon stretched out on the ground ready for the operating. In that manner he would be held till everything had been accomplished. Then the ropers would ease up their reatas, shake open the loops, and the calf would scamper to its feet. On big heavy stock a team might rope and hold by both front and hind legs.

The last ranch I worked with, up on the Mt. Hamilton range, handled their calves in a different manner. Before we started, a few of us made up a bunch of piggin' strings to be used in the corral later on.

187

Then the ropers lassed their calves, generally by the hind legs, dragged them near the fire, and the bull-doggers then hog-tied them with those strings, and there they were left till the operators got to them. Sometimes there were as many as eight or ten patients on the ground peacefully waiting their turn.

The Texas way is a little different. Rim-fire saddles, short grass ropes, hard and fast. The roper dabs his loop on the calf he wants and the experienced pony just wheels methodically without seeming to care much what the answer is, and starts back for the fire with a steady, nonchalant walk and paying no heed to the bawling, plunging, protesting thing at the other end of the thread. A couple of sweaty bull-doggers are waiting for the victim, and when he arrives the head man goes down the rope, flops the calf to the ground, puts his knee on its neck and takes hold of the uppermost front leg, bends the lower part back sharply and holds it in that way. In the meantime the flanker has also been busy, seating himself on the ground right at the calf's tail, one foot hooked just above the point of the hock on the leg nearest the ground and pushing it forward, grasping the uppermost leg in his hands and pulling it back. This is the regular conventional clinch for calves and it's a perfect hold.

When a roper drags in a calf, the bull-dogger, if he's at all experienced, shouldn't have much trouble flopping the small and medium calves. In a general way, he reaches over the calf's back, takes a double handful of loose hide, lifts the calf up on his knees like he would a bale of hay, and then gets out from under. All this in the twinkling of an eye, and the little critter comes down flat on his side with a wham! The attending bull-dogger then swarms all over him and before that calf can find what's left of the breath that so suddenly departed he finds himself stretched out in that helpless hold, or snugly hog-tied and equally helpless. Of course there are many, even among the little fellows, that are as limber and elastic and peppy as a pack of firecrackers

188

in action; and if they can get a leg or two to hit the ground first when they are slammed down, they can give one of those steel-spring squirms that only a calf seems master of, and the chances are they'll clown themselves out of that situation momentarily. They can cause many a laugh all around, and funny words from the bull-dogger. If the calf is big there's also a way a clever cowboy can flop it with the tail hold. In both the first way mentioned and the tail hold, individual cowboys have individual ways of doing it. In the former it has got to be quite a studied art, especially with the rodeo show contestants where seconds and fractions thereof count in the distribution of the soup coupons at the end of the day.

With big calves, a good roper who has any regard for the groveling, sweaty bull-doggers, should see to it that he brings them theirs roped by the hind legs. When a calf arrives that way, sliding along on its belly, all those hard workers have to do is to fall on it and get their holds without the real tough job of flopping them over. Right here let me state, and I speak from experience, when the calf crop runs big and husky, a waddie has a mighty good reason to feel doggone tired at the end of a day's work 'rasslin' the big, strong, snaky ones. And don't let anybody tell you differently.

I think one of the most amusing side sketches at a branding is that of a big calf being dragged in by the hind legs, sliding along so sedately on its belly in a cloud of dust. Tail first, head pointing astern with that silliest of silly expressions. The mother cow with all concern follows after for a ways, shaking her head with "moos" of misgiving; the calf answering in stilted "baas," or just taking it all in with silent and foolish wonder.

In the old days of the open range where many brands might make up the day's drag, a smooth-working branding crew operated with much teamwork. The mounted roper noticed well the brand of the mother cow to the calf he was dragging in, and as he approached the chosen spot he might bawl out, "Here's a Hashknife, boys, take it away from me!" And when the bull-doggers had the calf stretched out, one might call out, "Tally, Hashknife bull!" and would call till the tally man repeated to show that calf had been entered in the tally book. This also gave notice to the marker and the cutter that another calf was ready and also to the brander which iron to bring along.

The marker would slit the calf's ears and dewlap, if necessary according to the way that brand demanded. At this operation he likewise generally saved a piece of ear and dropped it into a sack or any receptacle handy, that at the end of the day these might be compared in number with the tally man to check up on the correct count of calves branded. Very often the marker also attended to the castrating. If not, it was done by another hand who just attended to that duty. All of the cutting work at these tasks was accomplished with ordinary, well-sharpened pocket knives. If disinfecting was done, there was another hand who generally followed the cutter with a bucket and swab. This, of course, should be done though it was not always practiced in the old days. There are many ranges where the danger from screw worms is a decided menace.

In some of the later outfits I've worked with I have seen as many as eight men attending to one calf almost at the same time, the whole séance not lasting over a few minutes. Two bull-doggers, the marker, the cutter, the vaccinator, the disinfector, the brander, and the tally man. That makes eight, not counting the roper, who seldom sticks around after his loop is opened and tossed aside. Everyone knew what they were there for; took their chores in turn; nobody got in anybody's way; and before you could say "Jack Robinson," that wild, free bull calf was let up without knowing what it had all been about, feeling a bit mauled and manhandled, to trot back to its mother, a branded, ear-marked, dewlapped, vaccinated and disinfected steer. Such was life for the range calf!

There was little lost motion in a well-directed branding, yet it was generally hot, dusty, dirty, singed-hair-smelling work; and when the last slick-ear was roped and thrown and attended to, and the straw-boss waved to the boys that the job was done for the day, it's an even bet the bull-doggers had to tuck their shirt tails into their pants and wipe the grimy sweat from their foreheads on their dirtier sleeves. And as they forked their waiting ponies to lope back to the chuck wagon for a bait and a rest, they had a right to feel they had done a day's work.

When a branded cow changed ownership and the buyer wished to make a record of it, he would mark off the original brand with a running iron and then rebrand with his own. This, when legally done, was called "venting a brand." Illegal brand blotters and tamperers resorted to all sorts of tricks and devices to accomplish their objectives. It doesn't take any too brilliant a mind to change one brand into another: just a little ingenuity and fussing around. However, it did take considerable cleverness to do a good job that would readily fool the average man inspecting it. A hardened old brand was not easy to blend into another design without showing where two different operations started and ended. A real experienced man could, in most cases, detect on close inspection, where a brand had been worked over or run out. In a matter of last resort, the skinned hide was often used as a mute witness. They claimed that the original brand burned on a calf showed through on the inside of the hide to a certain extent that an alteration made on the mature animal did not. Sometimes the thieves blotted out a brand with a flatiron, and then rebranded. Naturally, a crook would be mighty wary about applying a recorded brand at such an operation, for the very appearance of a blotted or burned brand would make one curious. The only value it really had was that it was hard to prove what was the original brand, and the crook would just wait and abide his time till he felt he could get away with it, and then he'd run such stock out of that range and dispose of it where he might have a buyer that was very

191

short-sighted. And believe me, "brand myopia" was a very prevalent disease among certain cattle buyers. In the characteristic language of the range, this unrecorded brand was called a "slow brand."

Another trick the more cautious thieves used, was to find calves that might have eluded the round-up, and many did, and after cutting the earmarks of the mother on it, they'd brand with the legal iron just enough so it would burn off the hair and not scar the hide. Or the brand might be marked by plucking the hairs out with the knife and thumb. Then the calf would be allowed to follow the mother throughout the summer and it would be watched till weaning time, and then, if everything seemed right, the crook would brand it with his own iron and recut the ears to match. This calf was called a "sleeper," and I think the reference is very apparent and well-named. Of course, the crooks tampering and altering brands did not always get away with it, and as the ranges were infested with these parasites, there was much human blood spilled in the operations on both sides. Yet many a lucky rascal, with a clever running iron, laid the foundation for the future fortune that squeezed him into the respectable, pillar-of-society, God-fearing, psalm-singing classes. Many a grand household had closets sheltering skeletons that would rattle like hell if given half a shake. But conditions were primitive on the old ranges, and one had to live hard and fast to survive. The degeneracy of softer civilization had not as yet set in. Then, too, on those lawless frontiers the flotsam and jetsam of humanity sought sanctuary after the Civil War. What could be expected?

Trailing through the Indian Territory in the late nineties, we camped near a ranch where they were branding the year's crop of calves. It was late in the season and the calves ran big and husky, and we watched the show with great interest and amusement. It was the most unusual branding I had ever seen.

There were three corrals strung along, all connecting with gates leading one into the other. In the first were gathered the cows and calves to be branded. The middle one, which had a snubbing post in the center, was used for the actual branding operations. The third was used to hold the cows and the calves after they had been branded. The boss was a Cherokee, as all are called in that country who have any infusion of such Indian blood, no matter how slight, and proud they are of it. In this case, however, I would never have suspected it, as he had light brown hair, almost blond, and a handlebar moustache quite rusty from sunburn and eating tobacco, and light gray eyes. He was doing the tallying, marking, and cutting. His young son manipulated the iron and gave a hand where he was needed. The ropers and bull-doggers consisted of three "Negro hands," all on foot. One had on a pair of disreputable old cowboy boots, and the other two were barefooted.

As I remember them, a couple were average, well-built bucks of medium height, while the third was a bull-necked clown, quite short and about as wide as he was tall, with a barrel chest and arms that Samson might have envied. His flesh was as tight and flush as a boar's, and I'll bet you couldn't have pinched it with a pair of pliers. He was powerful! Now, all these black boys took turns roping calves and let me state right here that they were above the average in handling that string; while one of them in particular, I have remembered all these years as about as sure-shot a corral roper on foot as I've ever seen. There were several saddled cow ponies standing sleepily outside the corrals but not a one within the enclosures.

I have always had great respect for a well-horned range cow with her calf when I'm afoot, and I wouldn't think of taking any liberties with them; yet these dusky rascals went in among them, roped their calves from right under their muzzles, and only once during the morning's work did I see a cow go on the prod when her calf bawled out as it was being dragged away. And that scene was funny enough, and remarkable enough to stay indelibly etched in my memory these many years.

When that cow decided to take matters in charge, she gave a bawl, lowered her head—and she packed a pretty pair of horns—brushed by her offspring, and made straight for the black at the other end of the rope. He awaited her charge crouched like a panther, yet never letting go the rope. When the infuriated cow reached him in her headlong charge, he made a beautiful side-step and slapped her over the nose heavily with the end of the rope. It was all as neatly and nonchalantly done as a torero's pirouette in the Spanish bull ring. The cow slid to a stop, turned like a flash, and came back on the prod. Once more the roper evaded the charge, but the struggling calf at the other end of the rope made it harder for him to maneuver this time. However, he never relinquished his hold on that rope. Again the cow turned, and then the pay-off to the whole show took place. Out of the dust that short black Samson appeared as if by magic, and before that cow could really get into "full speed ahead," he pounced on her, took hold of her horns in a bull-dogger's hold, and, barefooted though he was, brought her to a complete halt and twisted her head, though he made no attempt to throw her. He just talked to her with a patter that was a scream. Evidently this was no new situation to these toilers, for the third black now came into the picture, took her by the tail and gave it a peculiar twist, I never saw just how he did it, and the bull-dogger let go his hold. That cow gave a snort and hightailed it back into the bunch, deserting her calf like she had never owned it. That act was worth a grandstand seat in anybody's show.

But this is how they operated. They alternated at roping, and they'd catch their calves by the head or feet as fancy or the opportunity offered, for they were all good and could do about as they pleased with that string. Then, when the slack was taken up, the other two would also take hold and that calf would be snaked along at a jog whether it had been caught by the neck or was sliding along on its belly. No pony could have done a better job of hauling. The rancher's son tended gate and opened it to let them in to the central corral and closed it behind them. They would drag up to the snubbing post and half-hitch the rope to it quite short, though I never could see why, because a couple of them always threw and held the calf down while the boss tallied, cut and marked, and the son applied the iron. When through, the calf was released and as the blacks went back to the first corral for another, the mother cow of the calf just branded—and they were generally close to the gate—would be hazed through and allowed to join her offspring; and while the ropers were catching another calf, they would send them through the other gate and into corral number three with the fully branded herd. I can't say whether it was their regular routine or whether they were influenced by the audience they had that morning, but those black boys clowned continually at their work, with a running fire of small talk that was positively priceless . . . the real, old-time Southern darky patter, not the modern "blackface wisecracking." One of our outfit asked the boss why he used no ponies in the roping. He had appeared quite serious throughout all the work, but he grinned as he answered, "In this light work mah boys caint be hampered with no hoss."

I don't think there's any phase of the cowboy's yearly routine that has drawn more fire from the sob sisters and the "lovers of animals" than the branding with a hot iron and the marking of the ears with a knife. To meet these objections, if possible, many inventions with paints and acids and what-nots have been tried out. I don't know much about them, but I'm sure that when some other good system is found and its application is within reason, the cowman of the future will use it. He doesn't brand with any fiendish desire to inflict pain; he wishes he could get along without it. But, from what I hear, none of these substitutes seems to work out any too well for large-scale operations.

There are many outfits these days, especially smaller ones on well-fenced ranges, that do not earmark. And it's very possible that they don't need it. Of course, to the majority of outsiders earmarking is just another one of those relics of barbarism and absolutely unnecessary. However, let me add right here, that with big spreads and where different brands are liable to intermingle considerably, earmarking is as important, if not more so, than stamp branding. For instance a cowboy riding range in very rough and brushy country discovers a small bunch of cows on the other side of a deep, long ravine. The sides of this hazard are very steep, rocky and positively impassable for a half mile or more. He's a "stray man" from a neighboring ranch many miles to the north, and he's scouting for strays from his home range. Those cows across the ravine are broadside to him, but the ornery cusses, of course, are showing him their unbranded side and he can't read their identity. And yet you can bet your last six-bits every muzzle is pointed right at him in bovine curiosity and alarm, and every pair of ears is cocked up and cupped at him to catch the slightest hostile sound. Can that cowboy read those earmarks? Well, if he can't that waddie is blind and he shouldn't be wandering around unescorted.

If those cows had not been earmarked, he would have had to ride a half mile or more, to where he could just slide down a treacherous, steep ravine bank, with ten times the trouble to worm and scramble up the opposite bank, only to find that the critters he was interested in had high-tailed it for parts unknown. I'd say it paid to earmark.

And while on the subject of branding and earmarking, I doubt if there's one reader in a thousand who knows that these operations are *not* an invention of the "Cowboy West." They were branding and earmarking on our Atlantic seaboard over three centuries ago, sometime after the *Susan Constant* had brought our first stockmen to Virginia. The early colonists used the branding iron and the earmarks to denote ownership and the town to which the critter belonged. Nor was this system an American invention, for we have records of the same procedure being used in England earlier than the fourteenth century.

I think all stockmen must come from some sort of a universal mold. Listen to this Record of Registry for a personal cattle brand in New England, in the early colonial period. It has a crude, very crude and amusing angular sketch of a cow's head showing earmarks, to supplement the following text:

"December the 25th 1734 the ear-mark that James Frie Giveth his cattel and other Creatures is as followeth viz, a half cross cut of the under side of the left ear split or cut out about the middel of the Top of the ear, called by som a figger of seven."

There's another phase of branding that I have not touched on, and which is practiced to quite an extent on some ranches, and that is in chutes. This is a very handy contrivance for certain kinds of cow work, but there are many of the big-scale Spring round-up chores that can't be done in a chute. Anyhow, as long as cattle are raised for beef in large numbers on immense pastures, and until some other way of operating is invented, I think it's going to be hard to beat the roping cowboy and the fast, well-reined horse, to get the job done. But, of course, one can never tell; so this is no attempt at prophesy on my part. I've seen too many changes take place overnight, and today's range and today's cowpoke are not the same as those of yore. I'm not saying they are any better or any worse. I'm just saying they are not the same.

There was a time when a cowboy or cattle owner drifting over those unpopulated stretches of the old range, thought nothing of beefing a yearling or a heifer for the evening meal and the morning bite. They didn't even bother to skin it, but left it there with their compliments for the coyotes, buzzards, or other meat-eaters that might sift by. Cows were plenty, and man had to eat, and this was a proper and accepted custom. However, I guess it was perfectly natural and human for an hombre to beef one from someone else's brand than his own. Anent this question of free beef, I think more yarns have been told in Cattleland than about any other. "Why that old buzzard never tasted his own beef 'ceptin' it was in somebody else's camp." How many times have we heard that as a theme to character yarns for this or that local celebrity!

How some of those old-timers could remember and identify brands! Once they'd see an iron and place it, it would at once make an indelible record that would rest in the pigeonhole of their memories for immediate reference. It was a gift, and a mighty handy one, too, in the days of the open ranges and the long trails.

Comparing the old days with the new, I've heard so many folks state with a satisfied sigh of relief, "Well, thank goodness the old days of the cattle rustler are gone. That's one thing cattlemen should be thankful for." Or words to that effect. Well, I'll admit that's a fine line for a Thanksgiving Day thought, yet it would be much lovelier, and sweeter, and more comforting if it were only true. I haven't any statistics to show you, with percentages, and averages, and blah, blah, blah to prove just how the old and the new in cattle rustling stack up. Most statistics are a lot of bunk anyhow, and can be made to come out about as one wishes, and still "be telling the truth." They should be of value, yet they seldom are. Anyhow, let's get down to bedrock on this matter: There *is more* cattle rustling going on today than there ever was in the old times. Take it or leave it! And the rustlers may not be shifty-eyed cowpokes gone wrong, blotting a few brands with a hot cinch ring, and hiding the swag at the end of a blind canyon till sundown. Nothing like that. These brave lads are completely organized with high-powered vans, and trucks, and trailers; with code words for telephonic or telegraphic communication. They are financed and directed from a home office, and have regular established "fences," with all the faked legal papers and stage props to make the operations as safe as possible. It's a big business . . . a real, established going affair, just like big-time bootlegging of liquor.

198

This epic could fill a volume, and someone will write it up some day. But, for the scope of this effort of mine, I'll just stick to the old hay-burners for my material, and ditch the gasoline operators. However, I must add one parting shot, and that is to say that the old-timers were amateurs in the rustling game compared to these fair-haired modern lads. That's how civilization has purified the old Wild West, and made it nicer, and more comfortable for us all.

VI

 ell, I'd say it was high time we built ourselves a fresh smoke and got together on one very important topic: Just what kind of a horse did this Cowboy ride, anyhow? If we have saved the Pony palaver for the last, it certainly doesn't mean it's the least. Not by any stretch of the imagination! We might even possibly squeeze out some kind of cowboy without a cow, at least for a while; but we couldn't have a cowboy without a pony. No, sir! Why, that's what makes the darned thing function. You simply can't make a biped out of this hombre and still have him retain the character and usefulness he was designed for. Oh, yes, he could walk after a fashion and when it was absolutely necessary, but your old-time cowpoke saw to it that such a deplorable circumstance did not happen any too often.

So let us imagine ourselves back in those days when this range cow business was new to these United States, and let's have a good look-see and try to find out what was what in this matter of riding ponies.

See that cloud of dust boiling up over the rimrock? Well, that's little Joe, the nighthawk, hazing in the remuda. You waddies take down your lariats and we'll make a rope corral here, right from the chuck wagon. Those ponies are broken to a rope corral for temporary purposes. They've been taught to respect a rope early in life, and most of them do. Now let them quiet down a bit so we can give them the once-over, for, after all, a rope is only a rope. Now they've stopped milling around and snorting, and there they stand, heads up, ears erect, and eyes our way. Well, there's the remuda.

See that blaze-faced bay over there? Well, he'll go better than 750 pounds. Might go well over 800 when's he's hog-fat. Same for that sorrel next to him with the four white socks. They're big ponies. I doubt if that roman-nosed fleabitten gray will go much over 700. Looks big, but I doubt it. Anyhow, I'll bet the rest average around 600 pounds or a trifle better. The majority, I'd say, are under fourteen hands high. Oh, yes, they are all broken. That is, "cowboy broke." If you can saddle and bridle and get aboard one without too much outside help, he's broke. What may happen after that does not count: he's broke just the same.

These ponies are from Texas, and most of them from the northern part. Look 'em over well, for there's your cow pony. In other words, there's your Spanish horse, almost pure. He's the descendant of the horses Columbus brought over from Spain in the late fifteenth century, and landed them in the West Indies—Cuba, Hispañola, Puerto Rico, etc. When long-horned cows commenced to take on a little value, a few of the north Texas ranchers, in that good horse country, imported some bigger stallions from Kentucky or other parts of the Atlantic seaboard where they were paying a little attention to horse breeding. They graded up this Spanish horse, and before long those north Texas cow ponies took on a big reputation (and they deserved it, too), and were much sought after by outfits going up the long trails. However, we must also remember that many of those imported stallions they brought West had as their foundation stock the same little old Spanish horse. Don't forget that. It's a complicated business trying to unravel the breeding of all these various horses. So let's take a quick survey, just hitting the high spots, and see if we can get a better idea of just what the breeding was of those original cow ponies.

Of course, the first horses to set foot on New World soil were Spanish horses direct from Spain. There were no horses, wild or domesticated, in the Americas prior to their advent. In the old country, those hidalgos had been for several centuries continuously warring with the Moors, trying to expel them from the country they had invaded and occupied, and their aim was to drive them back across the Straits of Gibraltar and into North Africa, whence they had originally come.

Now, the Moor did his fighting and general gallivanting astride a very famous breed of horses—the Barb of the desert; and we all know that this breed is in great part Arabian. Naturally, throughout those fighting centuries, the Spaniards captured many and many of these horses and bred them for themselves. The Spaniards were good horsemen, and much of this most desirable stock was kept pure; yet it doesn't necessarily follow that all Spanish horses were pure Barbs. Not by a long shot. We must remember that most of these same Spaniards were in great measure from Visigothic stock, those Teutonic barbarians that overran Europe in the second and third centuries and eventually settled in Spain and southern France. There they were Christianized and, in turn, became the great bulwark to halt the all-grasping advance of the Mussulman. They were an equestrian people, and in their own barbaric invasion had fought as cavalrymen, and their own Teutonic horses were not entirely liquidated from the picture as the centuries passed. So, let me repeat that although there were many pure-breeds, it's a mighty wrong angle to assume that all the horses of Spain in the fifteenth century were Barbs. And it's a cinch that it was not alone the equine aristocracy that migrated overseas for the American conquest.

Those Dons, after several centuries of scrapping to free their country from the Saracen, finally got the nod from the Great Referee, and found themselves at last masters of their own country and as hard-bitten and salty an outfit of fighting muchachos as you'd care to see in anybody's corner. Why shouldn't they be? They had been in continuous training for several centuries. It was now poky business for them to hang up the old espada, the escudo, the lanza, and the tin haberdashery back of the kitchen stove, and take up the hoe to go messing around grubbing out weeds in the garvanzo patch as they were told now that all good citizens should. All this seemed like sissy business to this hard-bitten Don, and he was trying to kid himself out of the notion when along came this Cristobol Colon hombre with a lot of funny, new-fangled ideas which he finally sold to Ferdie and Isabel, the Spanish monarchs. They grub-staked this nut and the answer was that he discovered a spick-and-span new hemisphere; in fact, the other half of the world, though he never lived to know it.

Well, now, here was a brand new howdy-do! Unknown lands to conquer! Gold and silver for the picking! Muchacho! Don't tell me you could keep those lads on the farm after getting an earful of that stuff. Right off the pegs came the espada, escudo, lanza, and tin fighting duds. They had had hardly time to accumulate a decent crop of cobwebs.

Then they rounded up all the funny little old sailing craft they could patch up and put in commission, some of them no bigger'n a peanut, many without even a full deck. Yet into these tubs they stowed their ponies and away they splashed. When I stop to think of those human hellcats having the cheek to take horses over that rough and tough old Atlantic, maybe out for a month or more, in those crazy peanut shells, then am I convinced that either the Lord looks after the cheerful idiot, or the Devil takes care of his own. Take your pick, for it's an even bet. And they got away with it, too.

However, be that as it may, they brought over their horses and landed them on the various islands they settled upon in the Caribbean. That was the beginning of the horse in America. And here they prospered, though it was not until 1519 that the horse set foot on the American continent for that long permanent residence. That was the year when the intrepid conquistador, Hernán Cortés, set foot on the shores of Mexico, and commenced the conquest of an organized, militarily defended barbaric nation, whose trained soldiers could be counted by the hundreds of thousands. And this madman with but a handful of fighting fools! What a frenzied, mad adventure! It was only its positive madness that carried it through to a victorious climax. I consider it one of the greatest sporting events of all times; and still wonder how it was ever done.

It was the first time those hordes of Montezuma's soldiers had ever seen and encountered cavalry. Yet get a load of this—the mounted shock troops at Cortés' command consisted of sixteen horses. Did you get that? Sixteen horses! Now tell me they were not mad.

We have a most interesting and amusing record of those sixteen horses, handed down to us through all these centuries. The first horses on the American continent. I think it is of sufficient interest to insert it here in the very form, translated, that Captain Bernal Diaz del Castillo wrote it. He was one of that intrepid band of conquistadores.

"Captain General Cortés had a chestnut horse which died in St. Juan de Ulua: Pedro de Alvarado, and H. Lopez de Avila, (in partnership) an excellent chestnut mare, for exercise or service; after our arrival in New Spain Alvarado took her entirely to himself, either by purchase or by force: Alonzo Hernandez Puertocarrero, a gray mare called La Rabona (docked tail), well dressed, and of great speed: Cristoval de Oli, a dark chestnut horse, tolerably good: Francisco de Montejo, Alonzo de Avila (between them), a dark chestnut, not fit for service; Francisco de Morla, a dark chestnut, of great speed and well dressed: Juan de Escalante, a light chestnut horse, not good for service: Diego de Ordas, a tolerable gray mare, but of no speed: Gonzalo Domingues, an excellent horseman, a dark chestnut horse, very good, and of great speed: Pedro Gonzales Truxillo, a good chestnut horse, and speedy: Moron de Vaimo, a dappled gray, well on his haunches: Vaena de la Trinidad, a dapple, somewhat black; this horse did not turn out well: Lares, the good horseman, a very good horse, bright chestnut,

The Western Cattle Industry can trace its genesis to three contributions from old Spain: the durable Longhorn, the sterling Spanish Horse, and that human hellcat, El Conquistador, who brought them over.

JO MORA

of great speed: Ortiz the musician and Bartholome Garcia who had gold mines, a horse called El Harriero, one of the best that came over with us: Juan Sedeno of the Havannah, a chestnut mare which foaled in the ship. Sedeno was the richest man in our army, possessing also a ship, a Negro, bread, and bacon; some of which articles were indications of great wealth at that time, for horses and Negroes were hardly to be procured for any money."

There you are, and I think that's a mighty interesting record of our First Families in American pony ancestry. However, I don't think many of that stalwart bunch reached the stage of handing down much progeny for posterity. Theirs was a fighting schedule, and if you'll read this Captain Bernal Diaz' intimate history of the Conquest of Mexico I think you'll agree with me that after the terrific battles taking place during the campaign from the coast to the Mexican capital on the distant plateau, the activities there, the dreadful holocaust of "La Noche Triste" (the sad night) and the other fierce engagements before they reached the coast again, those original sixteen, the shock troops in every action, could scarcely have survived to be of much genealogical value to our cow pony. It is also curious, from another angle, to note that in this caballada there were ten chestnuts of varying shades, five grays, also varied, and one unclassified as to color though recorded by name. It is also of interest to note that those fighting Cavaliers were not averse to riding mares as their battle chargers. Of course, that's quite understandable, because that was the custom of the Moor, whose war steed was generally a mare. This preference for mares as battle animals with the Barbs, fitted in wonderfully with the schemes of colonization and stock breeding which generally followed the sword. All horseflesh was extremely expensive and difficult to obtain in those early Spanish colonial days, and I think they would have taken along anything that could navigate on four legs and neigh at the rattle of the corn bucket. Believe me, a horse was a horse in those days, prodigal as the supply and demand developed in later years. You may get a smile out of the mention of the two sets of partners owning and "operating" one horse in duet. I wonder if they matched pesetas or shook dice before each battle or steep hill to be negotiated. There's no record of this that I can find.

Many writers call the horse brought over by the Conquistadores, the Andalusian horse. Well, Andalusia was the last region in Spain to be held by Moors, in fact was the seat of the Mussulman Empire there, and even to this day bears much of their character, yet I would say that the Spanish horse that migrated overseas for the conquest, in those days, was just an average, general cross-section of the common everyday horse of the mother country. True, there were many pure Barbs in those contingents, but there were also as many that were not so pure. We do have records handed down to us, in their old manuscripts, of stallions sent to Mexico, for their colonizing projects, from the Royal Studs, the property of the Crown. This, on one hand, positively proves that the Dons never overlooked the importance of good breeding in their stock operations, but it doesn't necessarily make a thoroughbred out of that caballada that was so fast multiplying on the open ranges of the New World. Anyhow, we now have the Spanish horse, pure or unpure, from the late sixteenth century to the early seventeenth, taking out their American citizenship papers and settling down for a long, long stay.

And right here in this rope corral are his descendants, looking at you with independent eyes and distended nostrils. Three centuries of breeding by men who knew horses, and likewise by men who did not, and also of running free on the limitless ranges of those virgin lands, with all the varying conditions of climate and pasturage, did not contribute greatly to the refining or standardizing of a type. The difference from the scorching heat and aridity of the southwestern so-called deserts, to the lush grasses of the upper Pacific slopes, and the excellent summer ranges and heavily snowed winters of the upper Great Plains, all tended to form varying types in the process of evolution. They all had to rustle plenty for existence at certain times of year, either with the droughts of the southern country or the deep snows of the northern ranges. This, of course, served to weed out the feeble and unfit— the old survival-of-the-fittest stuff—yet was not exactly the grandest recipe for increasing the height and weight of the original ancestors. However, as they might have shrunk in size, they certainly gained in wind and sinew and fighting spirit and independence, till it produced a middleweight and bantam scrapper that could pack a forty-pound saddle and a husky cowboy all day at hard gaits, hard work, and over hard country. Then, when night came and he was turned loose or

207

hobbled to take a roll and rustle himself some grass, he could kick the hat off his rider's head just to keep his muscles limber and fit for the morrow's chores.

Take a good look at that pony before you and then let me add that you're gazing at *the welder of an empire!* And when I say that, I mean just that. Not alone the great Southwest, but an empire that takes in much of Canada, the entire United States, Mexico, Central America and all of South America. And that's glory enough for one little four-legged critter, I'd say. Many will say I am stretching it to include all of the United States. Well, let me tell you right here, much of the old-time horseflesh of the Eastern seaboard was the Spanish horse or had it for its foundation stock. He helped nobly to win the Revolutionary War, and he worked like heck on the other side, too, for the British and the Tories. That little rascal was versatile if nothing else.

There was a big commerce in horses during the Colonial days and when the nation was in swaddling clothes. They came in trading ships from the West Indies and also in great numbers in pirate bottoms operating in those waters. Yet not alone did he come by sea, for he was imported in great numbers also by land. Most of this business was done with the Indians who had better access to the horse-raising ranges of the Spaniards, either in legitimate trade or by plain, ordinary horse stealing. The Chickasaw Indians were the best known of these traders, and, in fact, the Spanish horse of those days was known in many sections of the country as the Chickasaw horse. The Choctaw Indians also figured greatly in this wholesale horse traffic.

To get a fair picture of the Spanish horse in relation to his advent and economic value on the Eastern Seaboard, we should have a little more than a hazy idea of how our pioneers operated there in the very early days, and after they had won their independence. The "West" was then an unknown land of far-flung horizons and deserts, while the known Atlantic coasts were of greatly varied topography, a large portion with the virgin forests reaching to the sea. The northern part was a rocky, rugged, pine-forested coast that was not a very promising region for stock raising. When man had to wrest his living from the soil, he had to literally carve his little farm from the rocky forest. Many of the mowings had to be cleared out of the dense forest, and the granite rocks and boulders sledded out by the hundreds to build the enclosing walls. Here the ox yoke was better than the horse. The early pioneer was a footman, a forest "still hunter" in moccasins, either in quest of meat or at war with that red brother who coveted his tresses, and this silently moving individual could not be bothered with a noisy horse. In other words he was not a rider. The big towns were located on the ocean front, and all transportation, wherever possible, was done by water. From town to town where the distance was great, travelers took the regular Packet Boats; and all the many rivers and navigable streams were used for passenger and freight transportation. The few coastal roads were miserable, and the stages operating over them were no inducement for the invalid who sought a restful pasear. It was all one's spinal column was worth to go stageing in those days. It was a six-day trip from New York to Boston; and it took three days from New York to Philadelphia. The mails, generally carried on horseback, were of little regularity and with no pretense at speed. All the interior freighting, with one exception which I shall soon mention, which could not be handled by flatboats or canoes, was done by pack horses, and most of these were Spanish horses. Farther south, in Virginia and the Carolinas, the backwoodsmen in the foothills of the Alleghenies, used quite extensively for packing, a small, fuzzy pony of Irish strain—some say Welsh. These were really ponies, while the Spanish horse, though we generally called him a pony, was really a horse. Even in his smallest phases he had none of the characteristics of the real pony. He was just a small horse: sometimes mighty small, I'll admit.

I stated above that most of the big towns were on the coast and mentioned one exception: that was in the State of Pennsylvania. There, a large migration of Germans had settled inland on the fertile valleys of the Susquehanna, the Schuylkill, and the Delaware. They were thrifty, industrious farmers and they made a marked success of their undertakings. They found that the Spanish horse, really only a saddle animal, was too light for heavy farm work, and so stood those mares to any stallions that had size. Although I could never uncover any authentic records, it is quite reasonable to assume that they imported some heavy draft studs from the mother country. However, they never made any pretense of creating a new breed; they were just reaching for size and weight in their horses for the reason that they were linking their interior settlements and farms with the city of Philadelphia by freight wagons. Roads of fair utility were graded, and before long an immense wagon trade took growth, starting from Lancaster and spreading out over this Pennsylvania hinterland. There it was that the Conestoga wagon originated and rolled to fame drawn by teams of six or eight horses. Naturally, the tallest and the heaviest draft animals they could find were used in this traffic. When you realize, as history tells us, that there were 10,000 or more of these freighters running out of Philadelphia, you may readily imagine that the breeding for heavier draft horses took on sizeable proportions. Philadelphia soon grew to be the chief town of North America.

In later years, long after this remarkable era was a thing of the past, the fame of the Conestoga horse took on a historical boom and they tried to peg that extraordinary equine as a distinct breed. He was supposed to be seventeen hands high and with all the desired conformation and points of an equine Samson. Well, he might have been all of that, and more, but I do know that many years ago I went into this subject as thoroughly as I could on the spot for a tentative Sunday newspaper article. The results of my research were that the fame of the Conestoga horse, in fact his very name, came from the wagon he hauled and not the wagon from the horse. I found that he was just the biggest, the heaviest, and the stoutest animal those Pennsylvania Dutchmen could buy or raise, without any knowledge, or, better said, attempt at building up a particular breed. They needed freight horses and they got them, mongrel or otherwise, just so long as they could lean into the collars and keep those wheels rolling. But we were full of those "horse booms" back East at certain times in the last century, and I only make mention of this one here to show that the foundation stock of those horses hauling Conestoga wagons was, in great measure, Spanish.

Quite unlike the cowboy's prodigality in the use of horseflesh was the curious custom of horseback traveling, especially in the northern states where economy was more of a virtue than in the South, called "ride and tie traveling." Two individuals starting out on a long jaunt would share one horse. One would start out and ride the horse a certain prearranged distance, and would then dismount, tie the horse by the trail or roadside, and proceed on foot. The other, who had started out on foot, kept on walking till he came to the tied horse, where he would then untie the partnership Dobbin, mount, and proceed. He would pass his companion and ride on to another chosen spot where he would dismount, tie, and continue on foot. Well, in this dot-and-carry-one manner they'd continue till they reached their destination.

When a man and a woman traveled on one horse, it was done in pillion style: the man riding in front astride, the woman sitting sidewise on the flank. Most of the saddle horses of Colonial times were Spanish, pure or graded.

In those early days there was another "breed" of horse that grew to great fame later on, though if ever there was a myth here it was. That was the celebrated "Narragansett Pacer." Back in the late nineties I also tried to delve into the make-up of this will-o'-the-wisp, but I got nowhere because I couldn't find a soul who had ever seen one. Yet I had one of those Rhode Island David Harums try to sell me a little fleabitten gray pacer with the *"guarantee"* that he carried the blood of this famous breed. I bring this horse into review only because the only dope I could dig up on him, apart from some perfectly worthless stuff, was that there were some excellent early pacers from that region, and that the originals had been imported there direct from Spain in a Yankee ship that had been exporting dried codfish to that country. I never got beyond that, which is pretty flimsy evidence, as I see it, on such a fancy fairy-tale horse as the Narragansett Pacer. However, legend and tradition have made this super-duper equine prodigy almost immortal. I always asked why this glorious breed was allowed to die out completely, and I was told that the demand was greater than the supply and that it was all sold out. Sold out to the planters in the West Indies. Sounds logical, doesn't it? Sounds more like good, old Yankee applesauce to me. But you may take it or leave it as you see fit.

Don't mistake this horse with the one they called the Virginia Natural Pacer. I don't know much about this animal, though I have found mention of it in several Colonial records, and I don't think it was put up as a distinct breed. I'd say it was just the best of the Plantation horse side-wheelers. He was a saddle horse, pure and simple, and those southern cavaliers were strong for easy gaits and good fast walkers. Look at the modern Tennessee Walker, for instance. I don't think there is the slightest doubt but that the original stock of the old southern saddle horses was this same Spanish horse, imported from the nearby Florida settlements or from the more distant Mexican or southwestern ranges. So, after all is said and done, I'd call this Spanish horse somewhat omnipresent, to say the least. Do you agree with me?

One of the questions I'm asked so often regarding these horses is how come such a vast, seemingly limitless extent of real estate, utterly devoid of horses, could be populated by them in such countless numbers and in so short a time. Well, that shouldn't be such a difficult question. In the first place, three centuries isn't exactly what I'd call so short a time. A lot can happen, brother, in that space of time.

However, to go into it a little more explicitly, though available space forces me to be sketchier than I'd like on this most absorbing subject, I'll just top a few of the high spots.

You see, after Cortés got through relieving the Indians of all the trouble of owning Mexico, and the main part of the fighting was over, the Spaniards busied themselves in exploiting the lands they had just acquired. Now stock raising was particularly suited to their temperaments and to those lands, and large ranches were soon established. These increased as the frontiers receded, and many of them were under the jurisdiction and management of the Church. And don't think that the religieux of the orders that operated there were all a lot of meek, psalm-singing individuals; many of them, even though fanatically devout in their religious fervor, were excellent stockmen and explorers, and the jobs they accomplished on those wild, dangerous ranges were no kindergarten efforts. Horses and cattle were raised in vast numbers, and the ranches kept spreading out more and more, continually eating into the unknown frontiers, and they had to fight for every inch of it, conquering the elements, the predatory animals, and the savage, warlike Indians.

To establish a great colonizing project and also on a cruise of exploration, Coronado departed from Compostella, on the Mexican west coast, with a very large expedition, for those days, and struck out for the great unknown. He had over three hundred mounted men under him, with a caballada of thirteen hundred horses, five hundred cows, and five thousand sheep. Some trail herd! As he proceeded into those new lands and he came to locations suitable for stock raising and ranching, he dropped certain contingents with the necessary stock and supplies to start up new haciendas.

Northward he went, and the story of his adventures and hardships and discoveries is one of the epics of American history. For our purpose here it is sufficient to say that, as he established ranches, the breeding and raising of horses commenced and continued to populate all that vast country. It is useless to state that many of these horses fell into the hands of the Indians, either by straying off their guarded ranges, or by direct thefts and raids. It was on this trip that the mention was made, which I referred to some pages back, of the stallions from the Royal Stud of Spain. There's no denying the fact of there being some aristocratic blood in the ponies that were seeded throughout those wild ranges. And this was a little over four centuries ago!

Coronado pushed on and finally landed in the country of the savage Comanches in the Llano Estacado of Texas. This was buffalo country and a new sight for Coronado and his men. He lost many horses in those herds and from stampedes, one, principally, due to a severe hailstorm. They had now come a long way, and they had not found the fabulous seven cities of Cibola which they had hoped to conquer and loot. So, after much discouragement, Coronado decided to return to his base in Mexico. He had in his party, however, a very zealous friar by the name of Padilla, who, in his fervent desire to save infidel souls and gather them into the folds of Christianity, asked permission of the Leader to continue to the land of Quivira. This he was given, and with two companions, a white man and his Negro slave, he pushed on with a remuda and reached a spot as far distant as northern Kansas or southern Nebraska. Here the friar was murdered by the Indians, though the white man with him effected his escape on a fast mare, and after an epic wandering finally did return to Mexico. The rest of that remuda acted as seed in those far ranges. So, you see, we are commencing to get a start: Mexico with its steadily increasing crop and then all this equine broadcasting throughout what is now Sonora, Arizona, New Mexico, Texas, Kansas and even into Nebraska.

Just about this same date, another Spanish expedition of exploration was taking place under the leadership of Hernando de Soto. We find him in Florida in 1539, and then hear of him trailing through Georgia, Alabama, and Mississippi. He was on a quest for gold, thinking those lands might yield precious dividends as Mexico and Peru had to others of his compatriots. But he found sterile prospects for the treasures he sought; though he did find plenty of trouble with the Indians. He treated them most severely and had a continual fight on his hands, losing heavily in personnel. He did discover the Mississippi River, and, finally, while descending it to reach the Gulf of Mexico, he was taken with a bad fever and died at the mouth of the Red River. He was buried in the waters of the Mississippi that the Indians might not find the body and wreak their vengeance on it. He broadcast plenty of horse seed throughout those Southern States on that pasear, and make no mistake about it.

However, by far the greatest mass planting was done by the Indians. As the great stock ranges were established and strung out all over that vast Southwest of ours, and the years rolled on and on, the numbers of the horses raised multiplied in a way that seems incredible unless you take out paper and pencil and begin to figure out a good average breeding table and see what you get. It's like compound interest. Anyhow, in due time there were thousands and thousands of horses on those vast ranges, and the Indians who had been stealing them when they were scarce, now had easy pickings, and this same pony created a complete transformation on a race of human beings.

The popular conception of our old-time Indian was a naked, painted, feathered gentleman with a long lance and a hide shield cutting all kinds of didos on a bare-backed paint pony, or shooting arrows from under that pony's neck, showing no more than a toe hold on t'other side. Well, that's all founded on fact at that, though there was a time when this same gent was nothing but a grass crusher with his own two feet. He traveled on foot, and he hunted on foot, and much

215

of his light impedimenta he packed on the backs of his dogs, or on a travois of sticks hauled by these same animals. Of course some of the heavier stuff was juggled by the squaws. That's quite a different picture from the popular one of the Great Plains Indians, isn't it?

Well, the Indian commenced to steal the Spanish ponies, and he learned how to ride. At first he liked to eat them, but later he found that pony was of much more economic value under him than inside of him. With him he could run down the buffalo and hunt him on even terms. He could pack heavy weights on him with great speed and mobility. His whole life was changed as was his entire economic structure. Do you wonder he grew very fond of that pony? From then on, his dream was to acquire them in great numbers. Well, they didn't cost him anything but cunning, courage, and a good chance of getting his hide drilled with lead. But he was accustomed to that kind of gambling, and it seemed a mighty good bargain to him. So he kept on stealing and augmenting his herds, till the Red Brothers farther to the north of him decided they'd like to cut in on this business; and so they, in turn, commenced to steal from him. Then the desire for ponies, you might say the absolute need, commenced expanding to the north more and more, and one stole from the other. It wasn't theft to the Indian; it was just the regular, accepted booty of warfare— the prize for courage and cunning, their great standards of life. They were warriors, pure and simple, and it doesn't take half an eye to see that it couldn't take long to populate the entire West with ponies under those standards.

With few exceptions, the Indians knew little or nothing of horse breeding, especially in the early stages of their horse acquisition, so, in due time, the size of the Indian pony, as a rule, did not compete with the one raised by the white man. The truth is that in the old days and even up to my time as a boy, any western pony that measured thirteen hands or under, and wasn't branded, was an Indian pony even if he came from the planet Mars. It made no difference; a small western horse was an Indian pony regardless. The truth is that this same Indian pony, as far as blood lineage went, came nearer to being of the original Spanish strain than the cowponies that were being graded up from bigger stock.

To my way of reckoning, the Spanish horse should have been called the American horse. He certainly rated that honor. He was the very first equine to set foot on American soil, and his get populated practically the entire hemisphere. In most sections exclusively at the start; in others enough to leave a foundation for future breeds. For example, in the United States, he may claim exclusively all the Southwest, the Pacific Slope, the Great Plains, and the "early" Southern States. In the Middle West and the Atlantic Seaboard he donated his blood in great measure to most of the horseflesh of those regions at the beginning of their "horse history." His blood is found in the foundation stock of the Thoroughbreds, The Standard Breds, Morgans, and that popular Plantation horse of the South. Even in the one they called the Canadian horse in early days you'll find the Spanish blood in his foundation. And so, down the entire length and breadth of the Americas to the end of the Pampas where the "Criollo" still reigns to this day.

Yes, that pony crowding away from your lass rope in the corral there is truly the welder of an empire. What other horse can challenge that claim? His stout back and tireless legs have carried nobly their human burdens in knitting together and gallantly forging that wild frontier of limitless horizons into the organized, civilized lands we now call our American West. This was never a footman's job. It took cavaliers to do it.

Now, what's in a name? In the early part of the nineteenth century, another of those "horse booms" oozed out of the East about a grand new breed, the American horse, which had been developed, and which was the "all purpose horse" par excellence: saddler, draft, pack, and driving roadsters. According to his promoters and boosters, he could do anything but wash the kitchen dishes. Well, let me repeat, it was all hooey, for it was no breed at all. Imported European draft stallions or any cross-breed that would give weight might figure in the pedigree. No records were kept, no attempt was made, and they bred back and forth and up and down, but the bunk about this American horse continued as a sales talk, with even the patriotism stuff that the name implied brought in to boost the breed, which was no breed at all to start with. Where is the American horse today? Well, he isn't because he never was. So what's in a name, anyhow? The title American Horse should have gone to this little welder of an empire we have before us. It isn't that he had so gallantly earned it; it's that he is the only logical candidate.

In the West we knew this critter as the Western Horse, the Western Pony, the Cow Pony, the Bronc or Bronco, the Mustang, the Cayuse, the Stock Horse, the Stock Pony, etc. This name business is always a tough one to unravel. Today you may go from one end of Cattleland to another in a matter of hours at the controls of a sky whizzer; but in the old days the distances were tremendous, and its various "corners" so isolated one from another that folks living in them coined words of their own and even gave differing interpretations to things they did. They often dressed differently, and rode differently, and worked stock differently. In certain sections the horses they rode were Cow Ponies; in others they might be Cayuses; in still others, Mustangs. Well, let's try to break down some of these names.

Take, for instance, the name Bronco. Sometimes it's spelled Broncho; why, I don't know. The word comes from the Spanish direct, meaning rude, rough, untamed. I have always applied that term to an unbroken horse. When a horse has been broken he positively ceases to be a bronco. I just couldn't apply it to anything else. Yet many writers call the cow pony a bronco, as a type or breed of horse. Of course there are many writers who do not know what a cow horse is, but I have heard the term applied wrongly by a few who should have known better.

Take the word "mustang." That is derived from the Spanish "mesteño." This is rather a tricky word and quite confusing. For years I thought I knew what the word meant, then I looked it up recently in the dictionaries and found there was something wrong somewhere. Here's what I found: One dictionary said, "belonging to the Mesta . . ." So I looked up the Mesta and found it was the Union of Stock Raisers. Now another dictionary says, "That which belongs to the Mesta (Mex). Wild and *without owner*, as applied to horses, mules, and cattle." Well, how can they be wild and without owners and still belong to the Mesta or anybody else? However, no matter what the word may or may not mean in Spanish, in the vernacular of old Cattleland I had always thought of a mustang as the original Spanish pony, whether he was running wild or after he had been broken. I know I'll meet sharp criticism from some on this, for the term "mustang" is in the majority of places applied only to the wild pony that has not been under human control for generations. But it's all a matter of habit. Early in life I was with those that used the word for the original native pony, and it's hard for me to change my viewpoint. Besides I'm not thoroughly convinced that I'm wrong, anyhow.

The word "cayuse," so popularly applied to the old-time pony in many sections of the West, came from those that applied that name to the good ponies raised by the Cayuse Indians of the Northwest. They were pretty good ponies, spectacular in color markings, and I guess some people, when they got to those ranges, commenced to call all other native ponies cayuses. In some inexplicable manner the name stuck and took the public's fancy, and there you are. I, myself, often think of the little western pony and refer to him as a Cayuse. Yet I know I'm wrong. But names are funny things. They often take the

THEY# TRAIL DUST AND SADDLE LEATHER

popular fancy at the direct opposite of their intended meanings; yet, if they get rolling, like a snowball, they'll take on so you just can't stop 'em. I think the best example of this, as I mentioned in the early part of this book, is to call a Cowboy a Cow Puncher. You'd have thought the old-timers would have considered that a fighting word. Yet the word took hold of the popular fancy and it stuck. In succeeding years I think the cowboys themselves got to like it. At least it looks that way.

However, let's remember one thing: the original Spanish horse, the cow pony of the old West, is now practically no more. They started grading up, and some crosses took on the weight and size desired, and still kept, even gained, in speed. For flash reining, the kind "that'll spin on a two-bit piece," I think you've got to stop at a certain size and weight. For many years this type held down the range work, but in the last few decades the trend has been more towards the parade and racehorse type. At least that's the way it looks to me. Maybe it's all for the best, and that I'm all cockeyed and old-fashioned; but what a treat it is to watch a good stockman at fast work, forking a level-headed horse than can do his stuff on a loose rein and with his head low instead of on his rider's chest or fighting a martingale. It's hard to make this kind of a cow horse out of running stock or with too much hot blood. At least that's been our experience, and we've tried. It's true you need speed in a good cow horse, but you also should have a certain amount of phlegm and not too many hair-trigger nerves. That's why martingales and all those Rube Goldberg reining contraptions were invented. How I do admire watching a working horse that, after a hard run and a snubbing slide at the end of a taut rope, will hold fast intently yet quietly, while the rider runs down that rope with his piggin' string in his mouth, to wrap up a few hundred pounds of struggling cow meat.

The old-time cow pony has passed on, yet he served his purpose and he certainly served it well. As for that, so has his old-time bow-

220

legged rider gone; he of the handle-bar moustache and hogleg on hip. He too has gone. Conditions have changed radically, and the modern cowboy is doing his job, cut to the up-to-date pattern, just as well as it was ever done, if not better. Of course, in this I refer to the working cowboy only, not the rodeo artist. And I'm not belittling the latter one bit, either. He's a superb horseman, a show artist, but he does not necessarily have to be a good cowboy, though he often is.

Cow ponies, like human beings, had their own locality character-istics. I mean by that that a good, well-trained pony from the Plains might be a total loss in fast work over rough foothill country. He might be able to negotiate a prarie-dog town at full speed, yet shake and snort with fear at a real dangerous mountain trail that your hill-raised pony would take in stride without batting an eyelash. Then again, a pony that had been trained and raised in open country might be the worst kind of a dud working fast in real heavy brush. And, by the way, this brush fighting also applies to men. It's an art, and make no mistake about it. I'll never forget my first assignment popping brush.

It was many years ago when I was quite young and new at the game, and though, even then, I thought I had already popped a little brush, that experience made me realize what a shorthorn I really was after all. It all happened in southwest Texas, in the brasada north of Laredo on the Rio Grande; and it's a great kick I can get now harking back to those grand old days when youth was in the saddle and one day seemed no more alarming than the other. Well, I got my baptism of popping brush there and I'll never forget my reactions to it all.

I was on my way back to the States, after a fine pasear south on the Mexican plateau, and this time, like a bloated plutocrat, I was hitting the cushions on the little, old narrow-gauge "Nacional." In later years I made this trip, that is from Monterrey to San Antonio, in the saddle. On the train I made the acquaintance of two men, easily thirty-five or forty years my seniors, as jolly and agreeable a team to travel with as you'd care to meet anywhere. One was a Mexican gentleman, an hacendado from somewhere in the San Luis Potosí country, whom we called Don Enrique. I think his last name was Flores, though I feel a trifle hazy about it after this half-century interim. The other was a Texan by the name of Thad Harte who was what we might call a commission operator in horses, working principally out of San Antonio, Texas. He spoke Spanish to the last degree of perfection; that is, with all the mannerisms, inflections, and vernacular of the Mexicans. Don Enrique's English was exceedingly sketchy—I might say even a little worse than that. Therefore it naturally evolved that the official language of our conference was Spanish, which I spoke fluently.

They were on their way to Nuevo Laredo to consummate a horse deal of considerable size, and were traveling together in the little Pullman drawing room; and their functions from there were conducted with that "open house" hospitality of the old Southwest. The result was that between those two, a middle-aged American from our embassy in Mexico City, myself, and the oft-repeated visits of both the Pullman and train conductors, we surely made a serious raid on the porter's commissary supply of spiritum frumenti. Those buzzards certainly loved their tea, and I guess it was my youth that allowed me to gargle along with them and still stay on deck through the heavy weather. My ticket read to San Antonio, but long before we reached the Rio Grande at the frontier, I had accepted their invitation to join with their outfits in driving a caballada of four or five hundred horses from Mexico into Texas and to a railway shipping point. It promised a grand adventure to me and I looked forward to it with all the enthusiasm and anticipation of youth. Don Enrique promised, at least a half-dozen times with dignified, alcoholic emphasis, to mount me on one of the best stock ponies in northern Mexico. He'd insist, every time, just like he had never mentioned it before, that this pony was not the best, but that he had never seen a better one; and would always

wind up with, "Muy perrito! Muy perrito!" (Very doggie!) He had me
like a kid waiting for Santa Claus.

I traveled with a mighty light pack in those days, and all my
baggage was carried in a leather-bound canvas sack, built on the order
of a mail bag, and under lock and key. I had it with me at my train
seat, and when we rolled into Nuevo Laredo I had already changed
into my old riding clothes and boots, with my leggings, spurs, and
gloves rolled up in my double blanket as hand baggage. The Pullman
conductor took my bag along with him and later delivered it in my
name to the horse-corral office where I was eventually headed for in
San Antonio.

The three of us piled off the train at Nuevo Laredo where we were to
be met by a conveyance of some sort in which we were to be taken to a
ranch forty or fifty miles up the river. But, running true to form in
that delightful mañana land, there was no rig to meet us. This circumstance did not seem to perturb those two "simpaticos compañeros" of
mine. They knew everybody that had drifted to the station to watch
the train pull in and out; and before the conductor had called "All
aboard!" they had gathered up three or four amigos and were already
gravitating to one of those rendezvous where they dispense the merry
mucilage. I could see with half an eye that this was going to be a real
serious guzzling party, and I truly regretted it as I knew it would
prove a severe strain on my limited purse. I was after fun, experience,
and excitement in the saddle and not over a glass. I could do that any
time anywhere.

However, in a couple of hours the long-expected rig rolled up in a
cloud of dust in front of the Cantina. I guess the driver knew where
he'd find us. Here was an old-fashioned American buckboard, rather
long, with two seats, and a good-looking Mexican lad, about fifteen
years old, at the ribbons with four panting, thoroughly dusty and sweat-
caked little mules. The lad was Don Enrique's nephew, and after the

customary embrace and patting of backs so characteristic of those races, we learned that there had been considerable trouble at the home ranch with the caballada. Another large horse herd, heading for American markets, had trailed by and unexpectedly got away from the drovers and mixed up with "our herd," which was being guarded only by a couple of vaqueros at the time. It all happened too late in the day to give sufficient time to do any unraveling, so the job of cutting out and separating them into the original herds was a difficult one that was put over for the next day. There had been quite a bit of fuss and argument and almost trouble regarding quite a number of the horses as to which herd they really belonged. The trouble was that both herds were put up from many different brands, most of the horses heretofore unknown to the drovers. Bills of sale and other paper documents had to be produced and messed over before the whole affair was finally settled. So it was that the kid had been sent in at the last moment, and he stated that he had a few errands to do and then would have to drive out a few miles to borrow a fresh team from another uncle to be able to undertake the return trip at once. This loomed like a grand chance for me to ease up on the drinking, so I "generously" volunteered to help the kid with his chores that we might get going again as soon as possible. My services were gladly accepted and away we went, leaving the tipplers to their own pleasures for the time being.

The kid and I got along fine from the start, and he claimed I must have been some rooster to keep on drinking with those two fish. Anyhow, we drove out a number of miles to a typical little Mexican ranch and borrowed a new team of three little mules and one pony. The kid's aunt, when she heard that Don Enrique and Thad were on a real drinking bout, insisted we had to have something to eat, for she knew they'd never think of it while the liquor flowed. So, she warmed up some fodder, and the kid and I soon wrapped ourselves around a mess of chile con carne with rice that was mighty good; but, shades of the lower ranges, was it hot! I doubt if I could have enjoyed it so much had I been thoroughly sober, but the very fire of it worked wonders on me and did much to counteract the walloping I had been getting from old John Barleycorn.

It was getting very late in the day when we returned to town. After a lot of provisions had been taken on for the home ranch, and I had bought me a new maguey lass rope, the sun had set and a big moon taken the situation in hand. Don Enrique and Thad piled into the back seat with set smiles on their faces, their eyes a trifle glassy, their movements slow and measured; yet, to a stranger seeing them for the first time, they might have passed as perfectly sober. By all rules of what's what they should have been packed aboard on stretchers. What a team! And was the aunt correct in her surmise! Not a word about food was mentioned. Anyhow, we were off at last.

The kid had just driven in over forty miles and here he was, heading back without any rest. He knew that rough road like a book, and said that if he had had his own team he could have driven back with the reins wrapped around the whip socket. However, this fresh team had to be watched. The road was perfectly clear in the moonlight, and I drove for the first couple of hours while the kid dozed and rested; but at the end of that time, though the air was now cool and bracing, it got hard for me to keep awake. I, too, had had a tough time of it. But when I finally turned over the reins and slumped down into the seat, neither the terrific rough jolting that the road gave us nor the novelty of the new environment could keep me awake. I needed that sleep and I got it. Youth saw to that.

I was awakened about midnight to help water the team at a little ranch where I thought the dogs would gobble me up hair and hide. I had actually to fight them off with the whip and stones. Once more under way, I quickly went to sleep again, and though it was a couple of hours later, it seemed but a few minutes to me when I was awakened once more by the barking of dogs. We were swinging round to another ranch house where there was a light burning in one of the rooms. Here was the end of our journey. We had made those forty or fifty miles in mighty good time over miserable roads. I helped unhook the team and turn them into a corral, and then gave a hand unloading. Don Enrique was greeted by his brother who had tumbled out of bed to do the honors in decided deshabille. And, by God, if they didn't insist on having several snorts to celebrate the home coming. You would have had to hogtie me and snap a twitch over my lip to pour that poison down my gullet at that time. But the kid came gallantly to my rescue by asking for a hand on something or other. I got my blankets and bedded down outdoors back of the house, though the unsolicited camaraderie of an overgrown pup who had adopted me from the moment I set foot on terra firma there didn't help much to sleep away the couple of hours left before sun-up. That pup and the fleas.

It seemed to me but minutes before I was awakened. There was much activity, and five or six Mexican vaqueros rode in. After a hasty washup, I made over to an enramada where they were serving breakfast. Don Enrique and Thad were already there with eyes a trifle bloodshot, otherwise looking unbelievably fit. The kid and his father were there, and also a quiet, pleasant, middle-aged Texan who was Thad's foreman. He had been there several days, had inspected the herd, counted them, and accepted them for the boss after the shuffling they had gone through on the previous day.

The vaqueros wolfed their bait in fast time and rode away, and in a short time another bunch rode in for their refreshments. These had satisfied their inner cravings and ridden away before any of the others showed any sign of wishing to get under way. Nobody seemed in haste, and they sat around and smoked and talked horse at leisure. The kid dug up an old veteran Texas stock saddle for me to ride, and this we dusted off and overhauled. We cut and restrung the latigos, and replaced a disreputable old front cinch with a much better one. It had a good pair of Mexican bulldog tapaderos, and the seat looked very comfortable and so proved to be. Then they produced a much patched ducking jacket which showed by its scars that it had been there before. I had my own leggings, spurs, and gloves.

The remuda was in the corral and we soon stepped over to it. Don Enrique put his hand on my shoulder in his nice, friendly way, and said, "Don Pepe, there's your horse over there, the one I promised you. The moro. You'll never ride a better one. He's getting a little old now, though not so much in years as in hard service. Good horses don't last long in the mogotes. Hang your rope on him, he's yours."

I had never been so disappointed in my life, and, to tell the truth, I felt that the old man had put one over on me. I felt boobed. Not that I had exactly figured he would mount me on an arch-necked fiesta parade horse, but the one he pointed out to me was a far cry from the pony of my dreams. While the others milled around a bit when the men came into the corral dragging their ropes, he just stood where he had been, with alert enough ears, yet positively unconcerned. He was the most "impersonal" looking horse I had ever seen. He was of good blocky build, one of the biggest in the corral as he'd go around eight hundred pounds. He was a decided blue with black points and almost solid black muzzle and head. But as he stood there in all equine phlegm and stolidity, you felt like rushing out with a saw horse to prop under him, to keep him from sagging down. He stood on a pair of front legs that seemed to have such a bow in them that he gave the appearance of being about to kneel down and say his Pater Noster.

My first impulse was to spring some sarcastic wisecrack to cover my chagrin, but I quickly realized that, after all, I was but a guest and wouldn't miss the fun and experience that this all promised for anything. So I said nothing, and tried to hide my feelings as I went over to my saddle and took down the rope from the bow. This new maguey in that chill morning air, never having been uncoiled or stretched, was as stiff and kinky as a wire. I tried to shake out my loop properly, and of course felt that all eyes were on me to see what kind of a vaquero I was; though possibly no one paid the slightest attention to me. I went about it all as nonchalantly as I could, though if a kid ever prayed that he might make a good catch, I was that kid. I walked up quietly to the horses trailing my kinky loop, and though most walked away from me, my moro stood alert, yet perfectly still. When I got within ten feet I commenced talking to him quietly and walked right up, passed my rope over his neck, slipped the loop over his ears from the back, and led him away to my saddle. I adjusted my rigging on him and looked over my Rocinante and took inventory. Those funny front legs were not sprung or warped, but were as straight as one could wish. However, he had a couple of lumpy growths of considerable size on one leg, and several smaller ones on the other, about the knees.

The kid caught up a pony for Don Enrique and saddled him right close to me. "El Moro is a good horse," he said, "but this country is cruel on good horses. They get crippled up as fast as we can break them. We thought we were going to lose him last year when he got a coma thorn in his joint. Papa worked on him like he was a Christian, and he saved him. It's that long scar on his left knee."

"Is he well reined?" I asked.

The kid flashed his teeth. "Try him, and see for yourself."

I did try him later in the day and found he was positively tops. Some pony! Those unsightly blemishes were, after all, but the honorable insignia of his calling—a veteran brush popper.

We fussed around those corrals it seemed for hours, but I guess it was because I was so impatient to get going. Finally, Don Enrique trailed his spurs through the corral dust, swung into the saddle, and then we all did likewise. We rode but a few miles when we picked up the herd which had been under way for a couple of hours. It was being grazed along leisurely where the feed was good, and I'd say we made about fifteen or eighteen miles that day. This was quite a surprise to me as I had imagined this drive a much faster affair. Not that I had figured it would be a semi-stampede with snorting nags and much hard riding, but, without really trying to delve into details, I just had not visioned it as such a leisurely drift. That night we herded our stock rather closely and with a big watch. They were still a little concerned because they knew that the big herd which had caused all the trouble with ours was not so far away, although we were not following their trail. They had swung more to the north. We did not have a chuck wagon, though we did have a cook and two packed mules. We carried our own blankets back of our saddle cantles.

The next morning we were up before daylight and the herd was drifted along in the same manner, and we reached the Rio Grande before noon. Here we held the herd and then camped awaiting further orders. I think there was some delay waiting for the United States customs inspectors, or border patrols, or something of the kind, due, in part, to the presence of the other horse herd. The next day, well along in the morning, we took the herd over without any trouble, and once on Texas soil we changed crews. All the Mexican vaqueros turned back at this point and the herd was taken over by Thad's outfit of cowboys. Don Enrique and his brother continued with us, and I was sorry to say good-bye to the kid. He had turned out to be quite an amigo, and he had put me wise to much that was of great value to me later.

The next day was quite uneventful, very hot, and much of the way through mesquitales as thick as the hair on a dog's back. Looked like the stuff only a snake would care to negotiate, wiggling through on his belly. All in all, the day was quite monotonous. And yet, the day that followed was my red-letter day and one that I was not to forget for many a moon.

It was in the forenoon, and the weather was very hot. I was thinking seriously of taking off my ducking jacket, for that sun was working on my back in a way that seemed to make my spinal cord crawl. The road we were on was really nothing but a wide, cleared-out ribbon through the brush with wagon-wheel ruts showing in places. It could scarcely be called a boulevard by any flight of imagination. The mogotes on either side looked impenetrable.

There were three of us together and the herd was separated at this point; and though we often rode quite close on the tails of those ahead of us, they were at that time about seventy-five yards away. I'd say we were about in the middle of the herd; possibly a little nearer the head. It was quite dusty and we could not see the head of our column, especially as the trail was curving to one side and the brasada was very high at this location. Then of a sudden the braying of a burro split the welkin, and, though it's a mighty difficult thing for me to describe in written words, before we really saw any change in the actions of the horses ahead of us, it seemed we could actually feel a curious, silent wave of something or other surging down on us. Then every head with ears went up, and they started crowding and snorting, wild-eyed and excited. The pressure from ahead was getting stronger, and they would have run us down if we hadn't worked like beavers with our coiled ropes in hand and the broadside of our ponies. They were crowding and piling up on us, now in a perfect frenzy, and we were fast losing control when a couple of those wild-eyed brutes dashed into the brush and most of those ahead of us now followed suit. It sounded like a twister had hit that brush!

The cowboy next to me yelled, "We gotta ride like hell to head and turn those bastards back! You, Jim, stay here and try to hold that bunch behind us from turning into the brush if you can! Come on, Jo, it's up to you and me to ride like hell!"

With that he set spurs to his pony, wheeled him sharply, and started tearing a hole in that impossible brush. Before I knew what it was

231

all about, my moro wheeled like a flash, almost unseating me, hurtled himself into the thickest of it and started splitting that mesquital like hell-thrashing rats. Then followed the wildest, most dangerous ride I had ever had. In fact, as I think of it now, about as wild as any since.

The many years that have intervened since then, almost half a century, have decidedly softened my viewpoint on certain matters, and I have lost completely that hesitancy about expressing fear or anything else that might lead others to think that I wasn't a tip-top, rootin'-tootin', reckless, fearless cowboy. Yes, I have lost, in all these years, that false pride such as drives men to charge in battle when their knees are rattling like castanets and they are even lukewarm or decidedly averse to the cause they are fighting for. Just afraid somebody might call them yellow; somebody, perhaps, whose own soul is the color of saffron. So, I'll just 'fess up and tell you how I really felt when that brush-popping fool moro took me into the brasada. Had I been alone I almost think I would have reined up and let those frenzied dumb brutes go on their crazy way to hell. I felt my life was worth more to me than a bunch of ten-dollar fuzztails. Thoughts like these flashed through my head though counteracted by realization that I had asked for all this. Meanwhile that cockeyed pony under me now had his dander up and was tearing that brush like he was going to a picnic. In spots where the going just seemed absolutely impossible he'd hurl himself actually broadside with a curious side-winding wiggle, much like a football player runs and offers interference to a big opponent. Then again, in places where the going underfoot was particularly deep and tangled, he'd make headway with a series of violent crowhops just like he was bucking. He couldn't tear through, so he had to keep jumping himself out. Nothing, it seemed positively nothing, in the line of tangled, thorny growth seemed to daunt him. I had never thought such a performance possible.

Meanwhile, my companion was going through the same antics on his horse, but he was perceptibly falling behind. The thrashing bunch of wild-eyed, frenzied stampeders were tearing along about twenty feet to my right, the leaders but a few yards ahead of me. I had no time to think of anything but how to save my own neck. Brother, I was riding! That damned moro was going to head that bunch or show me up. Although I did not try, I doubt if I could have easily stopped him had I wanted to. I was all over that horse dodging sudden death, and I think I spent about as much time under his belly as I did on his back. My face was severely scratched and bleeding. Early in the fracas I got a whack on the head that made me wish I could retract my nob into a shell like a turtle, and I made the greenhorn's mistake of closing my eyes. For that I got a cruel wallop—fortunately it was glancing—that nearly tore my hat away from the barbiquejo. This blow really hurt me and I could have quit any moment. A thorny, slender branch crossed under my chin and nearly slit my weasand. I think my bandana and a quick parry with my gloved hand actually saved me from that fate. I was wishing all the cockeyed, dumb horses in hell, and the brasada along with them to roast properly.

We were just abreast of the leaders when, of a sudden, we burst out into an open prairie of considerable size in the midst of all those mogotes. Truthfully, I never reined that pony, I hadn't had time to think with my muddled head, but of his own accord and with a fresh burst of speed he wheeled over and nearly knocked a couple of those leaders off their feet. Those following piled up on us and I thought for a moment we were going to have a terrific mixup. But they all stayed on their feet, though there was a very noticeable slowup and change of direction. My companion now broke out into the open, and under quirt and spurs dashed past our slowed-up tangle and headed and turned those beyond us. We had stopped them before they got to the brush beyond. We had turned them. We felt we had the situation heading for a solution when another bunch broke into the clear-

ing above us, and, taking a chance, we left our half-solved problem and
rode hard to head the newcomers before they could reach the opposite tangle. We got there in good time and were definitely turning them
when the foreman and three cowboys broke in, and boy! Did they
look good to us! The six of us were now able to get some order and
quiet out of that mob; and when they had thoroughly calmed down
we tried to take inventory.

The heat had been terrific in that tangle of brush and thorns, and
with the supermortal exertions those ponies had had to apply to carry
us at top speed through that God-forsaken cover, they stood now in
dust-caked, dirty lather, heads hung low, with throbbing, heaving
sides, their hearts pounding against our legs as if they would burst
right through their ribs.

Some of us were a sight, and looked like we'd been put through a
meat grinder. Now that it seemed all over, at least temporarily, I felt
I would not have taken a thousand dollars for the experience, though
I would not have given two-bits for another. And yet this was but
a cog in the routine of these brush-popping vaqueros of the brasadas.
It's a hard life, and it's still harder on horseflesh. Those ponies never
lasted long at their best, and sometimes a bad thorn from the devil's
head, or a coma in certain parts of the anatomy might put a pony
out from all future usefulness.

The rider, who had been with me, asked, "What in hell started
'em off?"

The foreman answered, "We popped on to a nigger driving a team
of burros to a water-barrel wagon. One of 'em started to sing. That's
all. But if we can work them back carefully through the brush, I think
we'll get out of it easy. Only half of them stampeded, I think."

After a good blow we worked them back gingerly into the brush
and through it till we came out on the road again. Before long we
caught up to the rest of the herd which was being held in another

and still larger prairie through which the road ran. They had already counted their animals, and as we drifted ours in we counted what we had. It was found there were eight or nine head missing, and Thad decided to hold the herd there and send back some riders to see if they could gather up the strays. This they did, and they did not drag back till sundown. They had every one of the missing, but they just about killed three good horses in doing it. I doubt if it had been worth the effort.

While waiting for the return of the hunters, we had plenty of time to look after ourselves and our ponies, and fix those that needed fixin'. My moro had several nasty thorn wounds, but none of them, fortunately, in critical places. While I was doctoring him up, I just heard the cowboy, who had been with me in that mad race, talking to some others near him. "That new hand, Jo, he's a sure 'nuf brush-splittin' fool. Boy! That's a fast pony he's ridin'. I popped in ahead of him, but he just about had them bastards turned when I come out into the open."

Naturally, I had a fine feeling of satisfaction at hearing those encomiums from that seasoned vaquero, but I quickly came to and realized there was no use trying to kid myself. To that bunch-kneed moro belonged all the credit, and I was just lucky he didn't get me killed in doing the job. I came within an ace of expressing some such damned fool admission, when the advice my father gave me, when I first left home, popped into my head, "Keep your mouth closed and your eyes and ears open if you would learn among strangers." So I kept my mouth closed, and I did learn a lot on that drive.

I've often had arguments with old waddies, and with dudes too, over what cowboys I considered tops in Cattleland. Well, it's a foolish premise to start with, because, as I've stated time and again, all *good* cowboys are *good* no matter what their local specialties might be, and these certainly vary. However, from my personal experi-

235

ence and reactions, the brush-splitting vaquero of the old days in the mesquitales of southern Texas (I suppose they still do it) had about the roughest, toughest, most dangerous ground to run stock on of any I know. At least that's my sincere belief. It's almost a toss-up between him and the cowpoke that rides in the heavy chaparral hill country where it is very steep and rocky and rough. There, a stumble from a pony dashing wide open down a steep grade will catapult a rider fifty feet in the air before the rocks come up to receive him. However, he has the remembrance of that pure mountain air while in aerial transit prior to applying at the Golden Gate; whereas memories of that sizzling, thorn-lined brasada would not induce the proper thoughts to have while trying to crash the above-mentioned entrance. But it takes specialists for either of those chores, and if I appear to give a trifle of the edge to the brush popper, I'll just repeat the expression of an old brasadero I rode with when he said, "Hell can't be no worse for it's just as hot here." And that covers it to a dot. Apart from fighting the fierce thorns, just the physical straining effort of forcing a way through that all-enveloping tangle at full speed, when the sun is sizzling at the top rung, kills plenty of fine horses. What the thorns can't do, the sun can; and many and many a pony gets wind-broken or sun-struck. Don't think this is just something that *can* happen; it was what did happen continuously when running spooky cows in the summer. And they, too, plenty of them, just "up and died" if they got overheated in their mad races for liberty. So, little old Pony of the Brasada, here's to you: you were a real horse.

I've ridden in the campo of Baja California where the vaqueros wear leather hats and leather coats, and in place of chaps have "armas." These are large leather aprons, almost a whole bull hide on either side, fastened and hanging from the saddle horn to reach back and cover the legs and thighs of the rider, yet not attached to him. All this formidable armament to work a few ribbey, mangey cows and "lepey" calves in

Lacing the corsets on a scrappy one.

JO MORA

those cacti-infested deserts. It's all mighty picturesque and "so exciting," yet why fuss around with stock in those God-forsaken ranges is beyond me. I suppose those paisanos are as much entitled to beef as anybody else, and they surely earn it. But as for stock raising for a profitable business, I wouldn't give them six-bits for the whole shebang wrapped and delivered. However, they seem to like it, and they are entitled to their own desires. But let me whisper something to you right here in case you might forget it. That, too, is a following for specialists. You have got to be a trained cactus artist to hob-nob with that society of vaqueros.

And while on the subject of cowland specialists, I must not overlook another, and that is the cowpoke and horse that operate on the lava beds of northern California. It isn't a very extensive stretch of cow country, yet there are some good cow ranches on it; but unless you've seen with your own eyes the rocky carpets that the Devil himself must have spread there for the atonement of some mighty wicked ponies of the dim past, you just ain't seen nuthin'. Yet the modern horses have to pay for it, and they are mighty good ones which don't deserve this grief. I must admit I have never run cows on that range, but my son and I have hunted mule-tails there and enjoyed the fine hospitality of the SX Ranch, and lived at one of their outlying cow camps. To take a look at some of those "carpets," which are a complete covering of small, medium, and large volcanic rocks, is enough to give a shorthorn goose-flesh when he thinks of riding over them at anything faster than a mile-an-hour pace.

So, again, let me repeat, it takes specialists for certain sections of Cattleland. The ranges vary so radically in character that it naturally calls for different methods in the way of working stock. Men and horses must be broken and trained to local requirements, and the top hands and ponies of one locality might not be so hot in another, and vice versa.

Northwestern Waddie, on Palouse pony, riding winter range.

JO MORA

Now, if this old-time cowpony was colorful in his individuality and achievements, he certainly was not drab in the coloring of his hide. You may run the full gamut of the equine palette, and you'll still be within his color brackets. There were bays and browns and chestnuts and blacks and whites and grays, flea-bitten, dapple or iron. There were buckskins, line-backed, lightly or heavily zebraed, or running through all the variations even to golden-eyed. Paints or pintos of all colors and variations like tobianos, which is but a modern name in this country, recently borrowed from the Gauchos of the Pampa. Sabinos in all colors, moros (blues), grullas (mouse-colored), and palominos (cream with white tail and mane). Sorrels and palouses (apaloosas)

239

and roans of all shades. In fact, I'd say pretty near every color, or variation of it, was there to be found. If you can think of any I've left out, why just add them in, for it's a cinch they were there too.

In his evolution throughout the centuries, with the many hardships he had to endure, with his feasts and his famines, he might have lost some of the rotundity he possessed when he was hand-fed and groomed. And if in the place of certain curves he assumed an angle or two, it was just the result of toughening up and continual training. He was tough, reasonably fast, full of courage, decidedly aggressive, and could take care of himself in the clinches. He did his work on grass, and had to be taught to eat grain. And when the work was hard and continuous on a grass diet, he lost flesh. When he got too poor he'd generally be turned out to rustle up the lost upholstery, and a new pony would take his place. Horses were cheap and it often took plenty to do the job.

In size they ranged from little rats such as you'd find among the Tribes and which we called Indian ponies, to those in the eight- and nine-hundred-pound classes. I'm talking of averages, for you can always find the exceptions that prove the rule. I'll never forget riding at a rodeo (a round-up, not a show) on a Mexican hacienda way back in the heyday of the old Porfirio Diaz regime. One of the ponies they gave me in my string was about the smallest piece of working horseflesh I ever rode in real cow work. While we were saddling up in the corral, and during the fun and hilarity, I mounted the little peanut from a standing jump beside him, without touching foot to the stirrup or laying a hand on him. This was no pot-bellied, big-headed Shetland pony type. He was just a pocket edition of a real horse and in good proportion. They rode lots of small horses and mules on those ranchos at that time; though I never did think the work was as hard and exacting and rough there as it was on the northern ranges.

For real punishing work you should have more weight to your stock horses to stand up well under heavy saddles and husky cowboys. But

Giving that tobiano bronc a lesson with the "Fish".

JO MORA

I've also seen stockmen go too far in this weight-carrying quest, sacrificing too much in speed and action. Then, again, I've seen this modern craze for speed, speed, speed; and though there are exceptions, the majority turn out giddy headed, temperamental, excitable runners that aren't worth their keep when it comes to real cow work on the open range. It's there you need a level-headed working partner and not a rodeo-show "pony express" mount that needs three swampers waving gunny bags in front of him to bring him to a half stop.

One can go to all extremes in this matter of what is the best type horse for all-around cow work. I think the scales will soon turn to the medium weight, blockily built, "quarter-horse" type, with a good burst of speed and enough weight to stand the wear and tear of hard roping. Apart from the demands for certain types for different ranges, the matter of taste in the size of a riding horse is quite personal. I like a pony fourteen or fourteen two hands high, and not topping over nine hundred pounds; while my son, who is a better rider and horse breaker than I am, can't seem to get them too big. There is no accounting for tastes anyhow, and that's what makes the world go round.

With the passing, long ago, of the one-type western stock pony, ranchers have been breeding up and down and backwards and forwards in that laudable search for the "Better Cow Pony." When gasoline first came in strong and the farmers throughout the country took to it with a justifiable rush, the horse commenced to drop out of the picture more and more till it looked like he was headed for the museum cabinet along with the Dodo. Of course, the western stockman stuck to horses. I guess he had to whether he liked it or not, because the gasoline boys did not design and put out any sort of a cow-punching motorcycle that could operate on the rough ranges, up and down canyons and barrancas, split brush, or snub a bull at the anchor end of a lass rope. It still needed the little old hay-burner to do these chores.

So, outside of this western range stronghold, and the polo and show stock, the fate of the horse that really had to work for a living kept getting worse and worse. Then there came a turn in his downward journey. I don't know how much he has been reinstated with the farmers throughout the country, if at all, but I do know that of late years there has been a grand boom for the "western stock horse," and the western rig, and the Western way of riding. The ever-increasing number of rodeo shows, and the dude ranches mushrooming all over the old ranges, have done much to popularize the horse; and, like all good American booms, everybody started getting on the band wagons. It seems everybody had to have a pair of fancy cowboy boots, and did they get fancy! Blue-jean overalls with the bottoms turned up a foot were the real thing in the best circles. Sombreros got bigger and bigger and whiter and whiter. They couldn't get sufficient good saddlers to turn out the stock saddles necessary, and silver trimmings got as popular as cigarette smoking with the gals. Well, it's a cinch that with all this monkey business going on, the horse had to keep in step. So the horse booms started up, first for this color and then for that. Now for this breed, now for t'other. Societies were formed for every breed and color, with stud books, pedigrees, specifications, blue blood and whatnots. All good, healthy stuff for the horse. He was certainly getting back into the society columns. Now it remains to be seen what this will eventually do for the real western cow horse. Will a more or less standardized cow horse evolve from all this boiling pot, or will the devotees of the various breeds stick fanatically to their own choice? Some are going in entirely for Arabians; some for Morgans; some for running horses; some for thoroughbreds; and some for this and others for that. And that's what makes me skeptic about the outcome. With all this divergence of opinion, hundreds of these breeders are producing "western stock horses," breaking and riding them with western rigs, but in localities far from stock ranges, and where the sight of a wild cow might scare the colt to fits. It's for the operating stockman and the working cowboy to produce the cow horse. Only under the working conditions of the genuine cow ranch will the true cow horse be forged. It'll take some time to get the answer, though the way things look now I doubt if they're getting down to any sort of standard. After all, stockmen are just as individualistic as any of the dudes who follow fashions.

Harking back for just one parting shot at the little old open-range pony, uncurried and unbrushed, living on grass and shying at oats and barley, don't think that he didn't have the makings of an aristocrat. Many a flash-reined cutting pony forsook his native range in the gay nineties and rode the rails to the Atlantic, there to mingle with hoi polloi and the visiting Dukes and Earls. You bet he cut plenty of didos on those polo fields, to uphold the best traditions of his own West for speed, courage, and maneuverability. They made tip-top polo ponies, as the game was played in those days, and they got to know what a blanket felt like and a bed of straw a foot deep. Muy perrito! But they took to it like a duck to water. Tell me they didn't have aristocracy way back in their unwritten pedigrees!

Well, here we are getting close to the home corrals. I hope I have succeeded in giving you a fair idea of how this Cowboy looked and how he operated and what he wore in doing the job. That's all I started out to do. It has been done for those who never knew the old West, yet want to know some of the details. To the stockman this is an old story and it is not intended for him. In many places I have digressed from the mere description of dress and paraphernalia to express ideas of my own on the way of doing things. In this I know many stockmen will agree with me and many will differ. Well, why not? There's always more than one way to skin a cat, and it's only the bullhead that thinks differently. Anyhow, at my age, I've got to the point where I really do try to see the other man's viewpoint. As I said in the early part of this book, I'm mighty glad I knew the tag-end of the old West before it

"Dance, dude, dance!"

JO MORA

really got completely manicured and marcelled, and cow-towns grew into big cities. Yes, I'm glad I was part of it and could watch its evolution with extreme interest if not with complete satisfaction at the way it was heading. But there's no stopping the great surges of Destiny, any more than they could stop that long parade of longhorns as they trailed north from Texas to change the complexion of an empire. The railroad, the telephone, the automobile and trailer, the radio, the electric refrigerator, and even the airplane have made stock ranching a vastly different game.

The regime of the old Cowboy was fast and furious and short-lived. He was a marked figure in American history: and if he "was wild and woolly and full of fleas and hard to curry below the knees"; and if, at times, he was a hell-cattin', shootin' hombre either in his cups or out of sheer animal exuberance or plain cussedness or self-defense, he *was* an American creation. He left a character to the lands he "opened up" that neither time nor gasoline will obliterate in a hurry. With all his many faults he stands out windblown and disinfected from the white-livered gutter products that are shaping our destinies now.

Yet, who is going to worry about all this in another hundred years? I'm not, I can promise you that. So, adios, amigos! And, as we say when the boys are scratching the bad ones, "Stay a long time, Cowboy!"